WINNING
THE
VALUES
WAR
IN A CHANGING CULTURE

WINNING THE VALUES WAR

IN A CHANGING CULTURE

*Thirteen
Distinct
Values that
Mark a
Follower of
Jesus Christ*

LEITH ANDERSON

BETHANY HOUSE PUBLISHERS
Minneapolis, Minnesota 55438

Published by Bethany House Publishers
A Ministry of Bethany Fellowship, Inc.
11300 Hampshire Avenue South
Minneapolis, Minnesota 55438

Printed in the United States of America

Library of Congress Cataloging-in-Publication Data

Anderson, Leith, 1944–
    Winning the values war in a changing culture / Leith Anderson.
       p. cm.

    1. Christianity—20th century. 2. Christianity—North America—
20th century. 3. Christianity and culture. 4. Moral conditions.
5. North America—Moral conditions. 6. Christian life. 7. Values.
I. Title.
BR481.A53   1994
277.3'0829—dc20   94-38361
ISBN 1–55661–340–7   CIP

To
Charles and Lillian Alles
They have lived Christianly,
exemplified godly values,
and are known by their fruit.

LEITH ANDERSON is the senior pastor of Wooddale Church in Eden Prairie, Minnesota. He is a graduate of Moody Bible Institute, Bradley University (B.A.), Denver Seminary (M.Div.), and Fuller Theological Seminary (D.Min.). The author of several well-known books, including *Dying for Change* and *A Church for the 21st Century,* he has served as seminary teacher, conference speaker, missions leader, and as a member on numerous boards. He and his family make their home in Edina, Minnesota.

Contents

Using This Book
in a Class

RESPONDING TO the current debate on culture wars and the church's place in modern society, the author challenges the reader on a very different level than the political arena, the media, or radical protest. Anderson calls the church and individual Christians back to biblical values as the foundation for any genuine and lasting impact on their culture.

For new Christians or mature Christians, these chapters will inspire a fresh awareness of the values that matter to God and that ultimately will win the values war in our society.

Whether each member of a class has a copy of the book or not, the discussion leader can fit the material into a thirteen-week adult elective study by dividing the material as follows:

Lesson 1:	Introductory, with selections from Chapters 1, 2, and 3.
Lessons 2–12:	Chapters 3–14, one per week.
Lesson 13:	Chapters 15 and 16 to conclude the course.

Questions at the end of each chapter along with subheads within the chapters lend themselves to handouts for note-taking. Those chapter titles, questions, and subheads may be used without permission, but any portion of the text reproduced for group use requires permission from the publisher:

Permissions Editor
Bethany House Publishers
11300 Hampshire Avenue South
Bloomington, MN 55438
(Fax 612–829–2768)

Christians "do not live in cities of their own; they do not use a peculiar form of speech; they do not follow an eccentric manner of life . . . although they live in Greek and barbarian cities alike, as each man's lot has been cast, and follow the customs of the country in clothing and food and other matters of daily living, at the same time they give proof of the remarkable and admittedly extraordinary constitution of their own commonwealth. . . . They busy themselves on earth, but their citizenship is in heaven. They obey established laws, but in their own lives they go far beyond what the laws require. They love all men, and by all men are persecuted. They are unknown, and still they are condemned; they are put to death, and yet they are brought to life. They are poor, and yet they make many rich; they are completely destitute, and yet they enjoy complete abundance."

The Letter of Diognetus
Early Second Century A.D.

Chapter 1

The Whole World Is Changing

SERGEI KRIKALEV had convictions, stability, success, fame, and fortune. He was a member of the Communist party, a citizen of the Union of Soviet Socialist Republics, a follower of Soviet President Michal Gorbachev, and a highly privileged cosmonaut. He earned a lucrative 500 rubles a month.

In April of 1991 Leningrad native Krikalev was launched into space to orbit the earth for four months. While he was in orbit, however, huge changes collapsed the nation he left behind. Most frightening was the failure of the technical system that was to bring the cosmonaut back to earth. With no means of returning to earth, Krikalev had to stay in orbit for a total of ten months.

Imagine how he must have felt when he finally came home and stepped on solid ground for the first time in nearly a year! But home wasn't the same. His country no longer existed. Michal Gorbachev had been replaced by a previously marginal politician named Boris Yeltsin who was now president of the new nation of Russia. The Communist party was out of power and in disrepute. Krikalev's hometown of Leningrad had been renamed St. Petersburg. His 500-ruble salary was significantly reduced by inflation and now was not enough to buy even a hamburger at the Moscow McDonald's.

There was no turning back to the old ways whether he wanted them or not.

Sergei Krikalev's true story is a parable for the human race. All of us now living through the beginning of the twenty-first century are experiencing the greatest era of change in human history. Some have chosen to call this time a "hinge of history" because society as we know it is swinging in completely new directions. Our generation is like the Industrial Revolution, about which Samuel Johnson said, "The age is running mad after innovation, all the business of the world is to be done in a new way."[1]

Social analysts and commentators are struggling to describe and explain all that is going on. Some claim that there was more change in the first ninety years of the twentieth century (1901–1990) than in the previous nineteen hundred years combined and that there will be more change in the final decade of the twentieth century than in the first ninety years of the century. Others claim that human knowledge is doubling every two and a half years.

In 1993 there was a television special celebrating the twenty-fifth anniversary of the weekly comedy show *Laugh-In,* and it included clips from past segments of the show called "News of the Future." Comedians Rowen and Martin pretended to be newscasters in the distant future, telling the most farfetched and impossible jokes imaginable. In one of the segments from 1968, their news of the future had included predictions that Ronald Reagan would be president of the United States from 1980 to 1988 and that the Berlin Wall would fall in 1989. We now live at the end of a century when yesterday's jokes are today's history.

Our rapidly evolving society is like a large truck slowly increasing speed on a level surface. When the road turns into a downhill stretch so long and steep that the bottom cannot be seen, the truck's speed doubles with every mile. It's a thrilling

---

[1]Quoted in International Urban Associates newsletter (Winter 1993), 5.

ride for our pounding hearts, but our frightened minds wonder if the truck will not soon be out of control or blow apart because it was not designed to travel so fast.[2]

Yogi Berra, who always cleverly managed to capture the obvious, once said, "When you come to a fork in the road, take it!" There is a profound sense today that we have come to a fork in history's road, and one way or the other we must take it.

To pretend there are no changes will not stop change. It is far better to become modern sons and daughters of Issachar. One thousand years before Christ during a tumult in Israel, the people had to choose between loyalty to King Saul, who was on the throne, and David, who aspired to the throne. Both men had been anointed by God. Despite the civil war raging between the two men and Saul's threats on David's life, David insisted on remaining loyal to Saul and refused to kill him when he had the opportunity. Imagine the confusion of the average Israelite. How does one choose between two leaders God has endorsed? While we know from the vantage point of later history that David was destined to establish a great dynasty that would eventually lead to Jesus Christ, this was not so clear to David's contemporaries.

In 1 Chronicles 12:32 it says that "the men of Issachar . . . understood the times and knew what Israel should do." That's amazing. Their numbers were small—only 200 of them compared to the national population. That's often the way it is: only a few understand changing culture and know what to do. However, as inventor Charles Kettering says, "We should all be concerned about the future because we will have to spend the rest of our lives there."[3]

Changes in the World

The list of changes is so long that any description is bound to be hopelessly incomplete. They occur not only in world politics but also in population, religion, and individual lives. These

---

[2]Leith Anderson, "The Church at History's Hinge," BIBLIOTHECA SACRA, Dallas Theological Seminary, Vol. 151, 3–10.

[3]*Time*, special issue (Fall 1992), 2.

forces of change flow together to produce worldwide complexity, destabilization, and uncertainty.

The most profound political change has been the collapse of Soviet Communism and the end of the Cold War. For nearly fifty years after World War II, the Cold War kept the world in a polarized tension that produced amazing peace. Every nation had carefully defined its relationship to each of the two superpowers, the USSR and the United States. These giant nations moved money, weapons, and diplomats back and forth around the globe to keep loyalties in line. The end of this standoff was a dream come true for most non-Communists, although there has been an unexpected price to pay.

When the Cold War ended, a power vacuum was created that permitted ethnic, religious, and regional rivalries freedom to assert their influence and ideas without fear of being crushed by a superpower. This led to the horrors of civil war in such places as Yugoslavia and Somalia.

In Yugoslavia, where once there had been admired stability, there was now wholesale bloodshed among Serbs, Croats, Muslims, and Christians. Rival factions with animosities dating back for generations erupted into open conflict.

Somalia had previously switched its loyalty between the East and the West. With no superpower to dominate this poor East Africa nation, it succumbed to clan warfare and mass starvation.

At the same time, the largest waves of immigration in world history began. Millions of refugees flooded over borders everywhere in the world. Turks flowed into Germany; East Asians moved into Great Britain; Mexicans and Chinese entered the United States, pushing the immigration rate to 100 per hour in 1993.[4]

In response to these and other redistributions of the world's population, many nations are redrawing their national boundaries and searching for their place in a new world order. As a matter of fact, the United States has yet to determine its role in a post–Cold War context. Now that there is no rival for military

---

[4]*USA Today* (October 2, 1993).

dominance, the United States must decide whether to police the world or let evil forces take over.

Concurrent with the political destabilization, population explosion has increased global numbers from 275 million in A.D. 1000 to 5.5 billion in 1993 and probably 6.3 billion by the turn of the century. Present projections estimate the world population at 11 billion by A.D. 2050.

This portends far more than a mere shift in numbers. Europe and the United States are shrinking in percentage of world population and increasing in average age, while Africa, Asia, and Latin America are increasing in percentage of world population and decreasing in average age.

Another example of redistribution is the worldwide phenomenon of urbanization, which is depopulating rural areas and bloating cities. Rural towns are left with the elderly, while cities are filled with the young. As a result, megacities are unable to cope with the numbers, the crime, the need for jobs, the shortage of basic services, and the expectations of so many citizens. Too often this makes for social instability that risks everything from anarchy to totalitarianism. It is a volatile environment.

Another factor that is becoming more important and powerful is religion. Islam plays a major role in the political and social changes of Eastern Europe, the Middle East, Indonesia, India, and many parts of Africa. And major news events often relate to religion: Arab-Israeli conflicts and accords; the bombing of the World Trade Center in New York City; the United States government's showdown with the Branch Davidian sect outside of Waco, Texas.

Furthermore, many ancient faiths are growing in numbers and influence. Some call it a rise in fundamentalism that affects every religion of the world—Islam, Hinduism, Christianity, and even Animism.

World leaders are struggling to understand how to deal with new forces and new rules. The political lessons and procedures of the past often no longer apply or work. As strange as it seems, decisions were easier to make when the center of conflict was nuclear weapons rather than religious and ethnic differences in complex urban centers.

Aside from affecting countries, cultural changes also greatly impact individuals in ways beyond personal control. For example, consider the family wage earner who had a good job in the defense industry. Because of cutbacks in budgets, military bases, and defense contracts, he lost the job that he thought was secure until retirement. Because his skills didn't easily transfer to a different career with comparable pay, he now earns half of his previous salary. The pay cut has consumed his savings, lowered his lifestyle, strained his marriage, changed his children's college plans, reduced giving to his church, and lowered his self-esteem. Changes in the world have rewritten the script of his life.

When facing changes, people can either adjust or resist. Those who resist change sometimes desperately seek pieces of their lives that they can control. There is a sense that "I may not be able to control my world, my country, my company, or my family, but I can control my exercise, so I'll run six miles every day." Often this desire for control spills over into the church where members think, "We can keep the church the same as it used to be. At least then I'll have one spot of stability in my life." Not so! The church is also changing.

Changes in the Church

At the end of the twentieth century, the church in the West is facing signs of decline. Many of our largest denominations are shrinking, and the number of Western missionaries is at risk as the average age of career missionaries increases and the number and quality of those entering missionary service decreases. Global democratization has lessened the power and influence of traditional Christian institutions, including denominations, universities, seminaries, missions, publishing houses, and parachurch organizations. Disregard for the traditional teachings of the church is seen in the widespread practice of birth control among Roman Catholics and the reduced influence of the clergy among Protestants.

While the church in the West is struggling, the church in the East and in the Southern Hemisphere is on the rise. As a result, the center of Christianity is quickly moving in that direction.

Estimates of numbers vary, but some give a hint of what is happening. Conversions in South America are estimated at 10,000 a day;[5] 20,000 a day in Africa; and 28,000 a day in China. About 50,000 new churches are established each year in South America while about 50–60 churches close each week in the United States.

The People's Republic of China is a grand example of the growth of Christianity in Asia. There were an estimated one million Christians in China in 1949 when missionaries were expelled and the People's Republic was founded. That number shrank to around 200,000 by the end of the "Great Proletarian Cultural Revolution" in 1968. Now the most conservative estimates of Christians in China exceed 50 million, and many think the number is more than 75 million and may be as much as 100 million. That represents the greatest growth of the Christian church in human history.

These geographic and demographic changes of the Christian church are significant, for they mean that Westerners, with their deductive and rationalistic ways, decreasingly dominate church life and theological thinking. Third World Christians are concerned about justice, power, poverty, righteousness, and suffering. Millions of non-Western Christians are interested in experiential expressions of their faith rather than in the propositional.

When a group of American Christians, of which I was a part, met a group of young Indonesian Christians, the latter asked us two questions: "When did you become a believer in Jesus Christ?" and "What persecution have you received as a result of your faith?" We Americans were quick to answer the first question but had no answers to the second.

At a convention of mission executives in Colorado, we were, at one point, told to divide into small prayer groups. I joined three men sitting near me—all strangers. The last man to pray in our group offered an impassioned prayer for the people of China, the world's most populous country. What most impressed me was the end of his prayer when he asked God to

---

[5]Speech by Luis Bush at the National Association of Evangelicals Convention, Orlando, Florida (March 1993).

"protect the Chinese church from American Christians." I was stunned. I had been taught that the people of other countries desperately needed us American Christians. But this man was implying that the Chinese were better off without us.

The point of this story is not to debate the relationships between the Chinese and Americans but to illustrate that the church of Jesus Christ is doing better in other parts of the world than in North America. I heard one analyst claim that "the Spirit of God is sweeping the world, bringing huge numbers of people to Christ and the church, blessing as never before in world history—everywhere except North America!"

Changes in North American Churches

The church in North America has entered a period of crisis in some areas and change in others. True, there are some bright spots of effectiveness and growth, but they are offset by dark areas of ineffectiveness and decline.

Historically, American churches have looked to denominations and seminaries for vision and leadership. Large denominations like the United Methodist Church spread so much that Methodist churches outnumbered United States post offices and more towns have Methodist churches than have post offices. But the United Methodist Church has shifted from growth to decline.

Most American churches are small and rural, and an increasing number are not surviving. One factor is that the average age of members is rising. Also, many rural churches are suffering severely from the decline of rural population and rural economies. It usually takes an average Sunday morning attendance of 125 for a church to be large enough to support a full-time pastor. However, most churches have fewer than 100 in average attendance, and 100,000 American churches have fewer than 50 in average attendance. This makes for hard times and difficult decisions. Churches that have been at the center of community life are closing, not because the church was bad or the people don't care but because they are caught in the tidal wave of world changes.

Despite the decline in the number of churches, belief remains surprisingly high. For example, according to one poll, 67% of Canadians believe Jesus was crucified and resurrected; 66% believe Christ was the divine Son of God; and 62% believe the life, death, and resurrection of Jesus Christ provided a way for their forgiveness. Only 15%, however, claim to have had a born-again experience.

A fascinating example of the profound changes taking place in North American churches is reported in *Maclean's* magazine. One third of the 15% of Canadians who are evangelicals are Roman Catholic.[6] Typically we have defined evangelicals and Roman Catholics as mutually exclusive classifications. Today those classifications overlap.

Major centers of Christian influence are also facing big changes. Seminary enrollments, for instance, are declining as fewer young Christians are considering vocational ministry. In the past, the typical seminarian was a young male beginning his vocation or calling. Today, a large percentage of seminary applicants are women or middle-aged and older adults entering a second or third career. Also, rather than being men and women who are called to ministry, a number of seminarians seem to be there searching for direction and meaning in life.

Many of the parachurch organizations (youth ministries, missions, associations of churches and denominations, evangelistic organizations, radio and television broadcasters) that were founded midcentury or earlier are showing their age. They tend to be controlled by retirement-age leaders and board members who are reluctant to surrender control to a younger generation. Since many of these organizations have elderly donors, there is a fear of alienating them with innovations or newer methodologies. In fact, some of these donors attach restrictions to their bequests in an attempt to control the organizations from the grave. At the same time, these organizations have been slow to recruit younger leaders and contributors. This is a dangerous combination because it virtually assures the death of the organization or, if it survives, dependency on endowments rather than effectiveness. In some cases it is just as well if the ministries die out with the generation they were designed to serve. In oth-

---

[6]Mary Nemeth, "God Is Alive," *Maclean's* (April 12, 1993), 35.

ers it would be far better if renewal enabled them to effectively serve present and future generations.

Another of the unsettling forces at work in the changing North American church is that the center of influence is shifting from parachurch organizations to megachurches. It's not that parachurch organizations have lost all their influence or that megachurches have completely taken over. The shift may only be a few degrees, but it is still significant.

Megachurches are comparatively few. Out of the approximately 375,000 churches in the United States, there are probably 300 with an average attendance of more than 2,000 and less than 80 that average more than 3,000. While they are few in number, however, these large churches wield great influence. They have become the source of television programming, doctrinal teaching, musical style, evangelistic strategies, and educational methods.

Megachurches can be compared to baseball. The National and American leagues comprise a small percentage of the total baseball teams in North America. Most teams are based in schools, communities, camps, and summer leagues. But the major leagues shape how the rest play baseball. And so it has become with megachurches.

Two generations ago the greatest influence on North American Christianity was small rural churches. One generation ago it was parachurch organizations. Now it is megachurches.

One of the greatest challenges to all churches, however, is the shift away from a pre-evangelized culture. In the 1950s, whether they were regular churchgoers or not, most people knew the basics of the Bible and Christianity. Today, I meet more and more people who have no church background, have seldom or never attended church services, do not know that the Bible has an "old part" (the Old Testament) and a "new part" (the New Testament), and have no reliable notion of what Christianity is about. To evangelize or educate those who know so little takes more time.

Generational differences also impact the American church. Distinct generations have distinct characteristics. The pre–World War II generation has a delayed gratification ethic, thinks systemically, and seeks to impose its values on others. Baby boomers (those born between 1946 and 1964), on the other hand, want gratification much sooner, also think systemically but are more tolerant of persons with different views and lifestyles. At the other end of the line are baby busters (born after 1964) who prefer instant gratification, think eclectically, and are even more tolerant than their parents.

One of the significant differences between the generations is music. Each generation now has its own radio stations. Few, if any, stations would dare to mix the music of the big bands, early rock and roll, country western, rap, and hard rock. Less radical but equally divisive musical preferences have polarized the generations over church music. To state the case simply, older churchgoers think worship should be "quiet" while younger churchgoers think worship should be "loud." It is difficult to do both at the same time!

As old traditions decline or disappear, what should be done? That question stirs many opposing answers and, sometimes, nasty controversies. Many want to go back, insisting that the old ways were better. Others argue that the calendar progresses whether we do or not.

Unfortunately, many analysts cannot distinguish between doctrine and method, and they are found in every denominational and ideological camp. Traditionalists insist that retaining orthodox doctrines means avoiding modern methods. Modernists tend to throw out yesterday's beliefs along with their methods. What is most difficult is to retain the truth of yesterday while adopting the methods of tomorrow.

Church historian Martin Marty warns that "to give the whole store away to match what this year's market says the unchurched want is to have the people who know least about faith determine most about its expression." *Newsweek* religion writer Kenneth L. Woodward says, "The mainline denominations may be dying because they lost their theological integrity. The only thing worse, perhaps, would be the rise of a new Protestant establishment that succeeds because it never had any."[7]

This is a critical time for the North American church, and

---

[7] Kenneth L. Woodward, "Dead End for the Mainline?" *Newsweek* (August 9, 1993), 48.

its future may be determined more by individual rank-and-file Christians than by institutions and traditional leaders.

Changes and Christians

How are individual Christians to respond to the tidal waves of change? That has become a major issue at this hinge of history. The answers are many, which further adds to the stress and confusion.

Denial is a familiar but unsuccessful response. The favorite verse of those who deny change is Ecclesiastes 1:9, "There is nothing new under the sun." While it is true that there is nothing new to the activity of good and evil, there are so many new expressions of both that denial becomes impossible. There have always been wars, abortions, spiritual renewal, sinful decline, and variations of everything else we experience. But the rapidity of change, the ethical issues raised by modern technology, and the globalization of trends is different than anything encountered in the past.

Frankly, denial is yesterday's response. In my experience, fewer and fewer Christians deny that unprecedented change has become the norm.

Withdrawal is another age-old response to change. Monasteries have been around for centuries, havens for those who would withdraw from the world and society. For those who withdraw, the mentality is more important than the fortress. The Christian who does so tends to say, "All of this is beyond my understanding and control. I can't make any difference in the world. Sin is awful and powerful. My best strategy is to build a wall around myself and my family to keep out the changes and evil."

Christians are not the only ones who think this way. Faith Popcorn has observed this trend in American culture and called it "cocooning," which she defines as "the impulse to go inside when it just gets too tough and scary outside."[8] This trend is evident in the popularity of home delivery rather than going shopping, renting videos instead of attending the theater, home

---

[8]Faith Popcorn, *The Popcorn Report* (New York: Doubleday Currency, 1991), 27.

schooling rather than sending children to public or private schools, working on the computer at home instead of commuting to the office, plus the skyrocketing sales of security systems and handguns for home protection.

Popcorn takes cocooning a step further in what she calls "burrowing," which is "digging deeper, building ourselves a bunker."

> The talk is increased crime, AIDS, recession, S&L's, and war. In fact, war news resonates deeply in our heart's idea of home. We talk of "hardened shelters" and "sealed rooms" against attack. Americans are buying gas masks. The fear of terrorism keeps us huddling at home. Leave our cocoons? Forget it. Instead cocooning has moved into a newer, darker phase—breaking down into what we are identifying as three new Trend Evolutions: the Armored Cocoon, the Wandering Cocoon and the Socialized Cocoon. Cocooning is no longer exclusively about a place, but about a state of mind—self-preservation.[9]

Counterattack is another very different but popular response to the changes in our society. Those who deal this way fight against the changes and struggle for control of the culture. Strangely, the activists who are counterattacking take a wide variety of approaches and often don't like each other. They even attack each other over opposing strategies.

During the 1980s there was a powerful movement among conservative Christians to counterattack through political action. Much of this was aligned with the Republican Party and Ronald Reagan and, later, George Bush. Other allegiances included Jerry Falwell, Pat Robertson, and Pat Buchanan. This movement peaked and declined when the desired results were not achieved.

Other activists choose guerilla warfare tactics instead of trying to work through established political structures. Most famous are Operation Rescue and similar elements of the pro-life movement. Those who have lost hope for stemming the tide of change through traditional means counterattack through protest.

---

[9]Ibid., 29.

The purpose here is not to discuss specific people or organizations but to illustrate the widespread discomfort that exists regarding the changes of our generation, as well as the wide range of efforts used to deal with those changes.

Some want to turn the calendar back and make tomorrow more like yesterday. Others accept that there is no going back but are fighting to make tomorrow better than today. Some have given up hope for the world and their country and have focused on taking care of themselves. Still others are optimistic, trusting that God and the Gospel will triumph and succeed no matter what. They don't expect the changes to be overcome; they believe the changes are the means to God's better future.

In all of this clamor, fear, and excitement, however, there is a danger that what is least important has become the most important focus of attention. Rather than argue politics and philosophies and strategies, is not our highest calling to "live Christianly"? Holding fast to the values and actions of Christianity in the tumult of change is what it means to be a disciple of Jesus Christ. If we live Christianly, we become like Jesus Christ in our generation. Winning the values war is more about how Christians live than whom Christians fight.

In the prayer of John Baillie, the great Scottish theologian whose life spanned the changes of the last century (1886–1960):

> Make me wise to see all things to-day under the form of eternity, and make me brave to face all the changes in my life which such a vision may entail: through the grace of Christ my Saviour. Amen.[10]

---

[10]John Baillie, *A Diary of Private Prayer* (New York: Charles Scribner's Son, 1949, renewed 1977), 53.

Questions

For Thought:

1. Think of ways in which you try to maintain stability in your life (or in your church) in this fast-changing world.
2. In what ways do you accept change and "go with the flow"? Are there ways in which you deny change? How does that affect your daily choices? Your life goals?
3. With the increasingly complex changes surrounding you, have you fallen prey to "cocooning" or "counterattacking"? In what ways?
4. What issues of our fast-paced society are sidetracking you from living Christianly?

For Discussion:

1. Why is it so difficult for churches to retain the truth of yesterday while adopting the methods of tomorrow? What generational differences exert their influence?
2. In what ways have the complex changes in the world affected your church and community?
3. The Bible says that "the men of Issachar . . . understood the times and knew what Israel should do" (1 Chronicles 12:32). How can we gain understanding of our own times and know how to respond Christianly as we head into the twenty-first century?
4. What are some positive and negative effects that megachurches can have on society in areas such as television programming, doctrinal teaching, musical style, evangelistic strategies, and educational methods?

Chapter 2

Living Christianly

A SIXTH GRADE student in Albuquerque, New Mexico, came to class wearing a T-shirt picturing pigs in various positions of sexual embrace. The teacher, Donald Whately, told the student that the T-shirt was "offensive and unsuitable for school, maybe the entire universe."

The boy told his teacher there was nothing wrong with the shirt and that his mother had bought it for him. The principal of the school, however, supported Whately's directive, and the student was required to wear the shirt inside out for the rest of the day.

Donald Whately, who is president of the Albuquerque Teachers Federation, is no narrow-minded reactionary. He told the *Los Angeles Times:* "For some reason I find that little incident to be a great moral victory. I wouldn't want my daughter to have to sit in a classroom and look at a T-shirt with pigs fornicating on it."

After explaining that there is a growing broad-based movement among America's educators to teach the difference between right and wrong, he said: "I think what we need is a real

radical and rapid shift to moral principles that can be taught—
as opposed to this notion that values are largely in the eye of
the beholder—because society can't tolerate ambiguity."[1]

Researcher Michael Josephson says "a hole in the moral
ozone has blinded the youth of America." His research shows
that in the past year 33% of high school students and 16% of
college students have shoplifted. One third of high school and
college students say they are willing to lie to get a job, and three
fifths of high school students and one third of college students
have cheated on an exam at least once.

His research also indicates that many of the students lied
when answering the survey questions about whether they lie,
cheat, and steal.[2]

This breakdown of ethics and morality is not limited to high
school and college students. It is so widespread that we can
truthfully say we are facing a values crisis in America.

William Bennett, former Secretary of Education and a fellow at the Heritage Foundation, established his Index of Leading Cultural Indicators in 1993:

> It showed that since 1960, there has been a 560% in-
> crease in violent crime. There has also been more than a
> 400% increase in illegitimate births, a quadrupling of di-
> vorces, a tripling of the percentage of children living in sin-
> gle-parent homes, more than a 200% increase in the teen-
> age suicide rate, and a drop of 75 points in the average SAT
> scores of high school students. Today 30% of all births and
> 68% of black births are illegitimate.
>
> The U.S. ranks near the top in the industrialized world
> in its rates of abortion, divorce and unwed births. We lead
> the industrialized world in murder, rape and violent crime.
> And in elementary education, we are at or near the bottom
> in achievement scores.
>
> But there are other signs of decay, ones that do not so
> easily lend themselves to quantitative analyses. There is a

---

[1]Garry Abrams, "Movement Grows to Teach Moral Values," *Minneapolis Star Tribune* (January 1, 1993).
[2]Michael Josephson, "Study: Many Youths Feel Honesty Isn't the Best Policy," from
the *Los Angeles Times*, appearing in the *Minneapolis Star Tribune* (November 13,
1992), 1A.

coarseness, a callousness, a cynicism, a banality and a vulgarity to our time. There are too many signs of a civilization gone rotten.[3]

The popular observation is that everyone lies, many commit adultery, stealing is common, and cheating is everywhere. But, beyond that, there is the growing perception that such attitudes and behavior are okay.

Many Americans are convinced that if you don't cheat on your income tax, you will pay more than your fair share. If you are a virgin on your wedding night, there is something wrong with you. If you do not victimize others, you will become a victim yourself.

Sadly, the Christian community looks much like the rest of our society. Surveys often indicate little difference between the attitudes and actions of those who call themselves Christians and those who do not. Jesus' notion that His followers should be salt and light appears to be for another time and place. Our salt has lost its saltiness and our lights have grown dim or flickered out.

Perhaps we have bought into the prevailing notion that we have a right to happiness and that happiness will arrive when we get more of whatever we want. In other words, we place higher value on what we don't have than on what we do have.

In 1993 the United Nations formulated a twelve-point list of prerequisites for being happy. The list for each family unit included one radio, one bicycle, and one set of kitchen utensils.[4] For most Americans that sounds more like a prescription for unhappiness!

Australian social analyst Richard Eckersley maintains that the core of our problem is a fundamental breakdown in values:

> The modern scourges of Western civilization, such as youth suicide, drug abuse, and crime, are usually explained in personal, social, and economic terms: unemployment, poverty, child abuse, family breakdown, and so on. And yet my own and other research suggests the trends appear to

[3]William J. Bennett, "Commuter Massacre, Our Warning," *The Wall Street Journal* (December 10, 1993).
[4]*Time* (September 13, 1993), 56.

be, at least to some extent, independent of such factors. They seem to reflect something more fundamental in the nature of Western societies.

I believe this "something" is a profound and growing failure of Western culture—a failure to provide a sense of meaning, belonging, and purpose in our lives, as well as a framework of values. People need to have something to believe in and live for, to feel they are part of a community and a valued member of society, and to have a sense of spiritual fulfillment—that is, a sense of relatedness and connectedness to the world and the universe in which they exist.[5]

These are not the kind of statements we would have encountered in secular periodicals as recently as ten years ago. Increasingly, however, social analysts are calling for cultural renewal, acknowledging that the values of the past three decades have caused havoc, and that a spiritual renewal is sorely needed. As Eckersley adds: "The United States, the pacesetter of the Western world, shows many signs of a society under immense strain, even falling apart. Recent reports and surveys reveal a nation that is confused, divided, and scared. . . . Most Americans, one survey found, no longer know right from wrong, and most believe there are no national heroes."[6]

Values determine who we are and what we do. Examining our values confronts everything about who we are, what we believe, and what we do. Because they define us so clearly, therefore, Christian values distinguish the followers of Jesus Christ from everyone else.

Seeking Christian values may not be easy or comfortable, but it is essential. For just as America is doomed unless we have values as a nation, the cause of Jesus Christ is doomed unless we have values as Christians.

Defining Values

Value refers to worth. When we value something, we rate or establish its usefulness, importance, its general worth. In mon-

---

[5]Richard Eckersley, "The West's Deepening Cultural Crisis," *The Futurist* (November/December 1993), 10.
[6]Ibid.

etary terms, value is the price we assign to something.

In the TV game show "The Price Is Right," contestants bid to determine the value of merchandise on display. If you know what you are doing, you will say that a bottle of spaghetti sauce costs $1.79 and the new car costs $23,500. If you get them reversed, you not only lose the game but demonstrate your stupidity to millions of viewers. After all, what kind of idiot thinks spaghetti sauce costs over $20,000 or that you can buy a fully loaded Dodge Intrepid for less than $2.00?

Sometimes the contestants are asked to put four or five items in order from costliest to cheapest, such as a car, a can of peas, a microwave oven, and a trip to Tahiti. It is a game of values—deciding which is worth what.

Now, imagine playing the same game, but where the items to be valued are telling the truth, winning the lottery, loving God, and being promoted at work. Which has the highest value? Is it more valuable to tell the truth or win the lottery? Is it more valuable to love God or be promoted?

Most of the time we discuss values in terms of behavior, but we need to distinguish that behavior is *what* we do and the way we do it, while values explain *why* we do what we do. Values govern our underlying thoughts, attitudes, and decisions which result in behavior. Even though we can't see values, they are real and powerful, determining human behavior.

There is a sense in which everyone has values. It's just that we put different price tags on the same things. One person will lie to get a job, while another person tells the truth even when it means losing a job. One person would never have sex outside of marriage at any price, while a prostitute sells sex for $50 a trick. Everyone has values, just different values.

Brandweek is a weekly publication of the advertising and marketing industry, which one would expect to have little or nothing to do with values. *Brandweek*, however, publishes information about values that "drive consumer behavior." (After all, American values determine American shopping habits.) Claiming that the consumer "seeks a synthesis of extremes," the magazine charted a comparison between traditional values and new values in the American marketplace:[7]

---

[7] "The Yankelovich Monitor," *Brandweek* (November 30, 1992), 18.

Traditional Values	*New Values*
Others	Self
Discipline	Indulgence
Material possessions	Experiences
Work	Leisure
Commitment	Choice
Conservative	Liberal
Obligation	Entitlement
At home	Away from home
Mass market	Niche market
Save	Spend

Much has been said and written about the debate between traditional values and new values, and "family values" has become a code word for certain political agendas. The debate has been divisive—even among Christians.

Could it be that the divisiveness among Christians comes from failure to define what are truly Christian values? For example, which is more Christian, "commitment" or "choice"? If the commitment is to wrong values or the choice is to sin, both are anti-Christian. If the choice is to follow Jesus Christ and the commitment is to God's reign in our lives, both are Christian.

The debate could be lessened and believers united by focusing on values that are clearly set forth in the Bible rather than on those primarily forged by changing politics and cultural expressions. Central Christian values from the Bible begin with God and truth, salvation, godliness, faith, good works, love, fellowship, forgiveness, evangelism, suffering, prayer, and integrity. When we agree and practice these values, we are far less prone to the divisiveness that arises over differences in denominations, political parties, and cultural lifestyles.

What we value is what we love. Jesus said in Matthew 22:37–39: " 'Love the Lord your God with all your heart and with all your soul and with all your mind'. . . . [and] 'Love your neighbor as yourself.' " In other words, Jesus said, "Value God. Value your neighbor."

Compare this with 1 Timothy 6:10: "For the love of money is a root of all kinds of evil. Some people, eager for money, have wandered from the faith and pierced themselves with many griefs."

Money isn't the problem. It's the value we attach to money. The apostle Paul was telling young Timothy about people who valued money more than they valued Christianity. They took the money and left the faith and wrecked their lives.

Sometimes it takes an outside perspective to see what we think is really important. Dr. Ronald Iwasko, a veteran Assemblies of God missionary to South America, is one such person. In his present teaching role in North America, he is able to observe the popular American value system as both an insider and an outsider. Here's what Iwasko sees:

"Worth is based on achievement." This produces the desire for recognition based on achievement and promotes competition among believers, which results in alienation from one another. There is a sense of frustration, failure, and worthlessness if recognition is not forthcoming.

By contrast, the Bible teaches that "worth is based on birth" (Isaiah 43:1–7; 49:15–16; Luke 15:11–32; Ephesians 2:4–5; Titus 3:4–7).

"Determination + persistence + knowledge + resources + time = success in just about anything." This "can do" attitude produces a challenge to do the most difficult, whether or not it is the most effective or necessary.

The Bible teaches that "apart from me you can do nothing" (John 15:5; 1 Corinthians 3:10–15).

"To know and to do are really important things." This produces the emphasis on many books and much hard work—a feeling that we must know everything. There is no time for meditation, prayer, quietness, and solitude. So we study like crazy and are constantly active. Books line our walls, especially the "how to do it" kind.

Compare the Bible's emphasis on *being* (Romans 8:29; 2 Corinthians 3:18; Ephesians 1:3—2:22; 4:24; 2 Peter 1:4; 1 John 3:2).

"Education is the key to success." This produces the drive for more academic degrees. Teaching is seen as the chief task of missionaries and ministers.

The Bible says: Faith plus obedience is the key to *godly* success, whether or not blessed in material possessions and position (Ephesians 6:7–8; 2 Timothy 4:8; James 1:12, 25; 1 Peter 5:1–4; Revelation 2:10).

"Role Status." For example, the company president is much more important (valuable) than the janitor. This perspective ignores the fact that while the president's *role* may have much greater impact, his *value as a person* is no different than the janitor's. This view causes people to strive for position or for high visibility and recognition.

The Bible teaches that all have the same status in Christ, but different roles (1 Corinthians 12:12–30; Ephesians 4:11–16; James 2:1–10).

"Equality in everything is very important." This produces the demand for equality rather than equity and the need for more and more rules to protect personal rights.

The Bible tells us that God deals with us as unique beings, each according to his own individuality (Matthew 25:15).

"Money can buy the things that will achieve the status that will bring us acceptance so that we can be happy." This produces the desire for more and more "things," especially those that give us status in the eyes of others.

According to the Bible, only God can bring true happiness as the fruit of a close relationship with Him. Our happiness in this life is *not* paramount (John 15:1–11).

"Time is linear, proceeding toward a goal. Therefore, progress is paramount." This produces obsessive-compulsive people with workaholic personalities.

Jesus said that when He returns, the issue will not be progress, but readiness and faithfulness (Matthew 24:24).

"The individual is supreme." This produces the demand to do one's own thing and the subsequent fragmentation of the body of Christ. Life is seen as a pyramid, and many Christians strive for the top.

The Bible says that the individual is important—but not at the expense of the group. There is to be diversity within unity (1 Corinthians 12; Ephesians 4:11–16).

Iwasko adds that "all of these are 'rules' by which we attempt to satisfy our basic needs, especially for significance, acceptance and trust. Though of the world, they have been adopted by North American Christianity, by and large. . . .

These values in the American way of life only produce alienation, aggression, competition, frustration and turmoil."[8]

While some may debate Dr. Iwasko's critique of North
American values, we cannot deny that he raises provocative issues for self-evaluation. Too often, we give little thought to defining or evaluating the values that are so much a part of our
culture and ourselves; instead, we assume them to be right.

Basis of Values

Many believe that all values are relative—that they change
depending on time and circumstances. It's sort of like buying a
Christmas tree. On December 21 the value is $6 per foot of
height. On December 26 the exact same tree isn't worth six
cents per foot. It's relative—it all depends on the date.

So, who decides? Obviously, people decide. Humans determine their own values. The human market for Christmas trees
sets the value on Christmas trees—and on everything else. Except the most important values are not about the price of
Christmas trees. The most important values are moral values.

Much of the moral crisis facing America today is rooted in
moral relativism. It is this relativism that says . . .

- Lying is okay sometimes but not at other times.
- Adultery may be wrong for some people and right for
  others.
- Someone who is young or beautiful is more valuable than
  someone who is old or unattractive.
- A picture that was obscene in 1934 is not obscene in
  1994.

For example, the Supreme Court of the United States ruled
that pornography is determined by community standards. But
different communities have different standards, and different
people in the same community have different standards.

When relativism is the rule, everyone is free to determine
morality according to individual preference or belief. Some say

---

[8]Ronald A. Iwasko, "The American Value System Exposed," unpublished lecture
notes, North Central Bible College, Minneapolis, Minnesota (1994).

homosexual behavior is normal and some say it is sinful. To some abortion is acceptable; to others it is abominable. It becomes impossible to hold a reasonable debate, much less come to any kind of moral consensus, when there is no agreement that moral absolutes exist. When the basis for values is relative and human, those values constantly vary and change.

Theoretically, then, we humans might one day decide that murder, rape, child abuse, and fraud are good, while truth, generosity, love, and fidelity are bad. In a world with relative values the price tags are constantly changing.

The opposite alternative is values that are absolute. This means that they are greater than our culture, our generation, our situation, or ourselves. Truth is always good. Murder is always bad. Faithfulness is a constant virtue and adultery is a sin—whether society agrees or not.

Some people who do not believe in God believe in absolute values. They think that truth is good because truth is good. Stealing is bad because stealing is bad. These are essential values that exist all by themselves.

Such persons may live wonderfully moral lives with very high values, but their logic really doesn't make much sense. Values are always tied to persons. Something has value or lacks value because it is or isn't worth something to somebody. It's like diamonds or gold. Somebody has to value diamonds to make them gems; someone has to say that gold is valuable for it to be a precious and expensive metal.

All of this brings us to God. Those who believe in God are driven to the conviction that God sets the values for our lives. What is good and bad, right and wrong, is determined by God.

Take a look at the Ten Commandments (Exodus 20). They are considered the greatest moral code ever written. These are not just ten good suggestions. They are far more than ten arbitrary ideas. They are moral absolutes based on who God is.

The Ten Commandments begin by saying that "God spoke all these words: 'I am the LORD your God. . . . You shall have no other gods before me. You shall not make for yourself an idol.'" In other words, God sets the values. God says what is worth more and what is worthless. He declares what is good and what is bad.

Who sets the prices at a major department store? Who decides what is more valuable and what is less valuable? Who determines the price of each piece of merchandise? We don't. Those who manage the store do. They decide and tag the merchandise accordingly. Our decision is to buy or leave.

The same goes with Christian values. They are set by God, not by us. He says that loving Him and loving our neighbors are worth an eternal fortune. He says that lying, stealing, cheating, and immorality are wrong. God sets the values. Our decision is to buy or leave.

Sports writer Curt Brown tells the story of a Chicago Bears football player who made the sports page because of his values. Since professional athletes are too often known for valuing money, sex, and power, it is interesting to find one who is different:

> Chicago fullback Bob Christian is a member of an elite club. He's a virgin. "I'm not ashamed of it," Christian told the *Chicago Sun-Times*. "It's out of choice and out of the grace of God that I'm a virgin. I'm very thankful I still am because when I get married I'll have something special to give my wife. I think that's God's plan, for you to be committed to one person all your life."[9]

He's an athlete who is a Christian not only in name but also in values.

Determining Christian Values

To be a Christian is to commit to Christian values. It means that we agree with God on what has worth. It means that we love what God loves and hate what God hates.

God has already told us His values. They are written in the Bible. God values justice. God values love. God values truth. God values forgiveness. God values the keeping of commitments.

In a sense, we can simply open up the Bible like a catalog and read the prices. Go for what God says is worth it. Avoid the cheap stuff!

---

[9]Curt Brown, "On the NFL," *Minneapolis Star Tribune* (October 9, 1993), 7C.

But what about specific issues on which God seems to be silent? The Bible does not contain the words abortion, pornography, or gambling. It does not mention anything about wearing T-shirts with pigs on the front.

The answer is to discover the values of God by knowing Him and understanding the values He has clearly taught. Ask, "What is God's likely purpose in this situation? What is most consistent with God's value of justice and law of love? What would Jesus most likely do in this situation?"

There is a strange little story recorded in 1 Samuel. It occurred when Saul was king of Israel. He and his son Jonathan commanded the army that was nearing battle with the neighboring Philistines.

> Not a blacksmith could be found in the whole land of Israel, because the Philistines had said, "Otherwise the Hebrews will make swords or spears!" So all Israel went down to the Philistines to have their plowshares, mattocks, axes, and sickles sharpened. The price was two thirds of a shekel for sharpening plowshares and mattocks, and a third of a shekel for sharpening forks and axes and for repointing goads. So on the day of the battle not a soldier with Saul and Jonathan had a sword or spear in his hand; only Saul and his son Jonathan had them. (1 Samuel 13:19–22)

How did Israel get itself into this position? Well, probably during peacetime it didn't matter. "So what if we don't have our own blacksmiths?" they probably said. "It's cheaper to let the Philistines do it anyway." But when peace turned to war, the Israelite army could not fight because the enemy had all the blacksmiths.

This becomes a parable for our times. If Christians and the church ignore the culture around them and leave values for society to identify, we are stuck when conflict comes. It is good to get along with our neighbors, but we cannot allow them to control the values by which we live.

When I was a boy I often heard my father quote one of his favorite sayings: "Your life is like a coin. You can spend it any way you want, but you can only spend it once."

Spend life well. Don't throw it away on that which is worthless. Spend life on the values that God says have great worth.

As Jesus put it, "What good is it for a man to gain the whole world, yet forfeit his soul?" (Mark 8:36).

Living Christianly

Politics will not solve individual or societal problems. Even though millions of Christians have diverted time and resources into massive political activity, the trend has not been reversed. Not even politician William Bennett thinks politics has the answer: "Our first task is to recognize that it is foolish, and futile, to rely *primarily* on politics to solve moral, cultural and spiritual afflictions."[10]

Some Christians have become politically aggressive and treat fellow believers as if they endorse sin because they do not march, petition, or politicize. At the other extreme are those who refuse to be socially responsible and criticize any political involvement as if it were proof of failure to trust God. While political responsibility is good and each must decide how much to be involved, let us not believe or give the impression that any political solution will create Christian values in society.

The highest value for a Christian is to live Christianly. That is, to live by the values of Jesus Christ regardless of the circumstances. Living Christianly is exactly the opposite of living circumstantially. Putting his life on the line, Martin Luther said, "Here I stand—my conscience bound by the Word of God—I can do no other."

Living circumstantially is an expression of relativism. Those who do so work hard at manipulating circumstances to their pleasure and satisfaction. They assign the highest values to health, wealth, success, and happiness. They do whatever the situation requires to get what they want at the moment.

Living Christianly is an exercise of faith. For those who do, the highest value is thinking and behaving like Jesus Christ. While circumstances are still important, they become the vehicles to live by faith. If we have wealth, we demonstrate the way Jesus handled wealth: "Though he was rich, yet for your sakes

---

[10]Bennett, op. cit.

he became poor" (2 Corinthians 8:9). If we suffer, we value a response like His: "To this you were called, because Christ suffered for you, leaving you an example, that you should follow in his steps" (1 Peter 2:21). This is the only way we can escape the tyranny of changing circumstance and win the values war.

What happens to us is not the most important thing in our lives; what is most important is taking the opportunity to live Christianly in whatever happens. This is true Christianity. This is the power of righteous living that turned the Roman Empire from a heathen nation to a Christian nation. It is what is happening in our generation throughout the People's Republic of China.

Politics can fail. Rebellions can be suppressed. Money runs out. Elections are lost. But living Christianly cannot be stopped. It is revolutionary. Even death cannot stop it. The early church historian Tertullian argued that "the blood of the martyrs is the seed of the church." The more Christians Rome martyred, the more people became Christians—because those who lived Christianly also died Christianly, turning the treachery of their enemies to triumph.

Eileen Cronin-Noe's life beautifully illustrates this kind of triumph over circumstances. She says: "My story begins between the 26th and 60th day after I was conceived. On approximately the 28th day, we develop limb buds, and this was also true in my case. Usually, the entire limb is developed by the 56th day. In my case, the development was hindered, and the agent which caused this was most likely Thalidomide."[11]

Thalidomide is a sedative that was prescribed to pregnant women in the 1960s, resulting in over 8,000 cases of birth defects in Europe and about 20 in the United States. Eileen Cronin-Noe was one of those babies. She was born with only a portion of her upper right leg and her left leg has only a small underdeveloped calf below the knee.

The response of Eileen's parents reflected their values and shaped their daughter's life:

---

[11]Eileen Cronin-Noe, "Thalidomide Baby Counts Blessings," *Minneapolis Star Tribune* (August 2, 1987), 1F.

Needless to say, there were monumental lawsuits brought by parents whose children were among [Thalidomide's] victims. A number of abortions were also performed on women who were informed of the possibilities.

For my parents, who did not have this knowledge, abortion was not an option and would not have been even if they had been aware of my condition. My parents believed that it was God's decision, and they were content with that decision. For this same reason, they did not pursue any legal action. For them, a lawsuit never would have addressed the issue.

Their belief has led me to accept, even prefer, things for what they are. Many people may find this difficult to believe. They feel lucky that amniocentesis is available to screen out babies born with less severe deformities than mine.

This thought frightens me, because I know that amniocentesis can't tell any parents what kind of child they will have. It can only tell what disability might exist in that child.

Amniocentesis could never have told my mother that I would have artistic talent, a high intellectual capacity, a sharp wit and an outgoing personality. The last thing amniocentesis would tell her is that I would be physically attractive.[12]

Eileen's parents' values informed and controlled their response to circumstances they never would have chosen. Eileen tells of difficult experiences, especially the cruelty of other children as she grew up. But she walks tall with artificial legs. She grew up taking ballet lessons, playing softball, dating, and fully enjoying high school social life. As a young adult she graduated from college and moved on to receive a master's degree and begin doctoral studies. She married and became a mother.

Circumstances never tell the whole story of our lives. Most of our biographies are written from the values we hold and contain our responses to those circumstances.

Imagine the impact on this nation and generation if Christians simply lived like Christ.

---

[12]Ibid., 6F.

Questions

For Thought:

1. If you died today, how would others eulogize you? By what values would you most likely be remembered?
2. What happens to us is not the most important thing in our lives; what is most important is taking the opportunity to live Christianly in whatever happens. In adverse circumstances, how often do you respond the way Jesus would?
3. How might you "simply live like Christ" in your present circumstances?

For Discussion:

1. In what ways are you most swayed by advertisers? What are the most powerful appeals?
2. What are some of the "new values" being forced upon us by changing politics and cultural expression?
3. What are some of the "worldly" values adopted by North American Christians that only produce "alienation, aggression, competition, frustration and turmoil," according to Dr. Iwasko?
4. Why will politics alone not solve individual or societal problems?

Chapter 3

The Greatest Worth

EVEN THOUGH the *Titanic* was called the unsinkable ship, it sank on the night of April 15, 1912, after it hit an iceberg in the North Atlantic. With a 300-foot hole in its hull, the ship disappeared in about two and a half hours. Out of 2,200 passengers, 705 survived. Only half of the needed lifeboats were available, and they were quickly filled with women and children. Most of the men died.

Recently I met a man whose grandfather was aboard the *Titanic*. As the ship was sinking, he offered a fistful of money in exchange for a seat on a lifeboat. He valued life more than money. And someone who valued money more than life gave up a seat but probably drowned with the cash.

It is all a matter of values: deciding what is worth more and what is worth less in life.

I've long been fascinated by what those who are dying or those who have had a close brush with death have to say about what is really important, about values. People in those circumstances usually talk freely about how differently they now view life. What once seemed worthless now has great value. They go on to tell me how little money and prestige really matter. They say that the irritations which used to upset them now mean nothing. They talk about the beauty of trees and flowers, their gratitude for every breath, the importance of relationships—and God.

I think of a man whose wife was desperately ill. During that time he was approached by friends who were deeply concerned about a proposed change in their church constitution. From past experience they expected their friend to share their concern and become involved. They were surprised when he said, "I have more important things to worry about."

Or I recall the words of a widow at her husband's funeral. The man had died of cancer in his early forties. She talked about the publications he had kept by his chair during the final months of his life. She held up a copy of *Gentleman's Quarterly* magazine and mentioned all the clothes left in his closet. She showed a catalog of Porsches and referred to the sports car in the garage. One by one she went through the magazines and books that represented a life of great success. Then she explained that as her husband's cancer brought him closer to death, the pile of reading material became shorter, until only his Bible and prayer book were left.

What if we could reorder our lives and values without the prompting of a heart attack or car accident or cancer diagnosis? If we could, what prize would be counted so precious that all of life would be given to win it? What would be at the top of our list?

Before we can even begin to sort out our life's priorities, we should consider the source of all that is good and valuable and worthwhile.

God Himself

King David of Israel had several close calls with death. Perhaps it was after one of these brushes with his mortality that he composed the stirring words of Psalm 145. The poem was rooted in his personal experience, but it became a famous song for his people.

I will exalt you, my God the King;
  I will praise your name for ever and ever.
Every day I will praise you
  and extol your name for ever and ever.
Great is the LORD and most worthy of praise;
  his greatness no one can fathom.
One generation will commend your works to another;
  they will tell of your mighty acts.
They will speak of the glorious splendor of your majesty,
  and I will meditate on your wonderful works.
They will tell of the power of your awesome works,
  and I will proclaim your great deeds.
They will celebrate your abundant goodness
  and joyfully sing of your righteousness.
The LORD is gracious and compassionate,
  slow to anger and rich in love.
The LORD is good to all;
  he has compassion on all he has made.
All you have made will praise you, O LORD;
  your saints will extol you.
They will tell of the glory of your kingdom
  and speak of your might,
so that all men may know of your mighty acts
  and the glorious splendor of your kingdom.
Your kingdom is an everlasting kingdom,
  and your dominion endures through all generations.
The LORD is faithful to all his promises
  and loving toward all he has made.
The LORD upholds all those who fall
  and lifts up all who are bowed down.
The eyes of all look to you,
  and you give them their food at the proper time.
You open your hand
  and satisfy the desires of every living thing.
The LORD is righteous in all his ways
  and loving toward all he has made.
The LORD is near to all who call on him,
  to all who call on him in truth.
He fulfills the desires of those who fear him;
  he hears their cry and saves them.
The LORD watches over all who love him,

> but all the wicked he will destroy.
> My mouth will speak in praise of the LORD.
>   Let every creature praise his holy name
>   for ever and ever.

The central assumption in these words is that every Christian value, everything of eternal worth, begins with God. He is loving, compassionate, generous, good, powerful, and righteous. God is bigger and better than everything else. All of life and all of the world is interpreted on the basis of the supreme value of God.

There are three primary ways for us to see and understand this: observation, revelation, and experience.

Observation involves looking at the world and universe in which we live. From the design we learn certain things about the Designer.

The December 28, 1992, issue of *Time* magazine carried the cover story, "What Does Science Tell Us About God?" In the article, writer Robert Wright said:

> One intriguing observation that has bubbled up from physics is that the universe seems calibrated for life's existence. If the force of gravity were pushed upward a bit, stars would burn out faster, leaving little time for life to evolve on the planets circling them. If the relative masses of protons and neutrons were changed by a hair, stars might never be born, since the hydrogen they eat wouldn't exist. If at the Big Bang, some basic numbers—the "initial conditions"—had been jiggled, matter and energy would never have coagulated into galaxies, stars, and planets or any other platforms stable enough for life as we know it.[1]

In other words, there obviously is a design, a plan for our universe.

Some highly sophisticated scientists have seen this and concluded that there must be a God behind the intricacies and balances of our physical universe. Many unsophisticated non-scientists who have observed natural phenomena have reached the

[1]Robert Wright, "What Does Science Tell Us About God?" *Time* (December 28, 1992), 40.

same conclusion: The God who originated the universe must be greater than the universe. In both cases, the even greater conclusion is that the Creator certainly must be more valuable than the creation. It just doesn't make sense to elevate a product to a higher level than the One who made it.

However, other observers have reached different conclusions. Some who examine our earth and the universe do not see the carefully calculated order; instead, they see chaos. They think there are more exceptions than rules and believe that scientific observation argues against God rather than for Him.

Still others observe the evil in the world and become confused or hostile toward God. How can they recognize God as good, generous, compassionate, loving, powerful, and righteous when so many suffer and die? Instead they devalue God.

Because observation lends itself to different perspectives and conclusions, it by itself is not enough to determine God's true value. Observation must be supplemented with *revelation,* the second means by which we discover God, the ultimate value. The best instrument for this method is the Bible, the record of God's revelations about himself. By reading His Word, we can learn specifics about God that we cannot see in the world around us.

In the Bible we are told that God created the universe, that God is personal, that God never began but has lived forever, and that God is good and wise and kind and powerful. The Bible also tells us that God is a judge with standards upon which He insists: He has expectations, He rewards, and He punishes.

The Bible repeatedly teaches that God is the greatest value of all and that everything else should fall into place in relation to the worth of God. It is the central principle of Matthew 6:33: "But seek first his kingdom and his righteousness, and all these things will be given to you as well."

Jesus was teaching the comparatively lower value of the things humans worry about—life, food, drink, and clothing. There is a hierarchy of values: Life is more important than food; the body is more important than clothing; humans are more important than animals.

Pagans, Jesus said, demonstrate a backward value system, constantly running after the less valuable. Christians have a higher value system because we "seek first his kingdom and his righteousness." When God is most highly valued, everything else fits into places of lesser worth. And we need not worry, because "all these things will be given to you as well."

We would not know any of this if God did not reveal himself and His value in the Bible. Observation alone could never figure it out.

Experience is the third means by which we learn about God. We have had encounters with God that shaped our understanding of who He is and what He does. Those experiences range from spectacular miracles that surprise us with God's grace to serious disappointments because God did not comply with our desires.

Observation and revelation without personal experience may give us correct answers that don't make any difference in our lives. This is at the very core of evangelical Christianity. Evangelicalism has always been experiential Christianity, which explains why evangelicals place so much emphasis on the born-again experience. Correct Christian doctrine without personal involvement isn't practical, isn't real.

Some Christians place primary emphasis on observation, some place primary emphasis on revelation, and some place primary emphasis on experience. Those tilted toward the rational and intellectual argue that God's revelation must dictate and control all experiences. Those tilted toward experience claim that their personal encounter with God is what makes the revelation alive and relevant.

Certainly all these elements are essential to rightly valuing God. Different emphases pressure us toward balance. However, the vast majority of new Christians are coming to belief through experience, not reason. Of the thousands of conversion testimonies I have heard, almost all detail a supernatural experience that influenced their conversion and high evaluation of God.

Understand that neither observation, revelation, nor experience determines or changes who God is and what He is worth. God is God, independent of our knowledge or experience of Him. If we never observed evidence of God, if God never revealed himself, and if we never experienced God, He would not be worth any less.

Another way to look at this is to consider human eyesight. I was born with astigmatism, which means that my eyes are shaped more like footballs than basketballs. Without corrected vision, everything I see looks distorted. But just because it looks distorted does not mean it is distorted. Some people are color-blind and some cannot see at all. But their faulty vision does not change reality.

In the same way, our distortions of God do not change God. He is perfect and of the greatest value whether we see Him that way or not.

Have you ever heard someone say, "If that's the way God is, I don't want to have anything to do with Him"? As if God is shaped by our choices. As if what we want makes any difference. God is God! His value, His truth, His desires do not depend on us.

God's value precedes everything because God precedes everything. Once upon a time there was nothing but God. He made everything that exists. Not only is God the most valuable, but all other worth comes from Him. Thus, any value we attribute to any object comes from God. Even our value as individuals comes from God.

If you sense that I am struggling for words to describe God's greatness, you are right. Why? Because it is impossible to completely describe His true value. There are no numbers or concepts that begin to rate what God is worth. He is so far out of our league and range that we cannot truly grasp His value.

It is like trying to comprehend $4 trillion of national debt. I looked up "trillion" in my dictionary and it gave two definitions: "(1) see number table; (2) a very large number." So I looked in the number table, which said that a trillion is a number with 12 zeros after it. That's a thousand billion! It is more than I will ever comprehend, more than I will ever see, more than I could ever spend, and certainly more than I will ever have. Then I noticed that a trillion is one of the smaller numbers in the number table. There are words I had never heard of, like duodecillion and vigintillion and centillion. A centillion is a number with 303 zeros after it in the American numbering system and 600 zeros in the British system. I imagine that these multiples can go on forever—an infinite number of zeroes.

And so it is with the value of God. My best words are limited to numbers like three, seven, and ten. But the value of God could be numbered in the centillions times centillions to the centillionth power and beyond. His value is infinite. Nothing else begins to compare.

God's value is already established forever. But that doesn't ensure that we humans rightly value Him.

"Treasure in Heaven"

A wealthy man once stopped Jesus, telling Him that he wanted eternal life. By "eternal life" he meant "the life of God" or "the life of eternity." It wasn't so much that he wanted to live forever but that he wanted to live like God.

> As Jesus started on his way, a man ran up to him and fell on his knees before him. "Good teacher," he asked, "what must I do to inherit eternal life?"
>
> "Why do you call me good?" Jesus answered. "No one is good—except God alone. You know the commandments: 'Do not murder, do not commit adultery, do not steal, do not give false testimony, do not defraud, honor your father and mother.' "
>
> "Teacher," he declared, "all these I have kept since I was a boy."
>
> Jesus looked at him and loved him. "One thing you lack," he said. "Go, sell everything you have and give to the poor, and you will have treasure in heaven. Then come, follow me."
>
> At this the man's face fell. He went away sad, because he had great wealth.
>
> Jesus looked around and said to his disciples, "How hard it is for the rich to enter the kingdom of God!" (Mark 10:17–23)

Jesus put this man's values to the test. He wanted to know which the man considered more valuable, God or money. Sadly, the rich man flunked the test—he chose his money.

The story says "he had great wealth." But no matter how

much he had, God is worth far more. Obviously, this man didn't value God for what He is really worth.

This man is not the only one who ignores God's value. James 2:19 tells us that even the demons know God's value, believe in Him, and tremble at His greatness. Yet they live in rebellion against God as if He were worthless.

When we devalue God, we add value to ourselves. Perhaps the simplest definition of sin is: to believe we have more value than God.

> For although they knew God, they neither glorified him as God nor gave thanks to him. . . . They exchanged the truth of God for a lie, and worshiped and served created things rather than the Creator. (Romans 1:21, 25)

Call it sin or call it stupidity. Either way, it is comparing ourselves and our possessions to God and living as if they possessed value greater than God.

Our generation has chosen to be self-centered rather than God-centered. We value ourselves above all. Our happiness, our pleasures, and our ways take precedence over everything else. Child abuse occurs because we no longer value children. Marriages break up and families crumble because we no longer value marriage and family. God is not central to our lives and decisions because we do not value God as highly as we value ourselves.

The results of our sin and stupidity are clear to see. We are not happier. We do not have more. Putting ourselves first has not brought personal fulfillment. Rather, failure to value God as God has resulted in epidemic unhappiness, moral bankruptcy, and personal misery.

God has infinite value, but that doesn't mean He is valued. That's where Christian values come in. A Christian is someone who values God above all. A Christian values God for God alone.

God Alone

When the Hebrew people entered the land of Palestine, Moses gave them advice that covered every aspect of life. In a sense, these words are a summary of everything else in the Old Testament.

> Hear, O Israel: The LORD our God, the LORD is one. Love the LORD your God with all your heart and with all your soul and with all your strength. (Deuteronomy 6:4–5)

Centuries later, Jesus quoted these words as the greatest commandment of all:

> "Teacher, which is the greatest commandment in the Law?"
>
> Jesus replied: " 'Love the Lord your God with all your heart and with all your soul and with all your mind.' This is the first and greatest commandment." (Matthew 22:37–38)

THE VALUE OF GOD: "Hear, O Israel: The LORD our God, the LORD is one." (In other words, the Lord is unique. He is one of a kind. He is valuable. He has unique worth. The Lord's value is unique.)

THE VALUING OF GOD: "Love the Lord your God with all your heart and with all your soul and with all your strength." (We should live up to that value.)

Do we get it? The greatest good of life is to recognize God for who He is—not for what He does (although what He does is wonderful) or for what benefits we might gain (although those benefits are huge), but simply for His greatness. And valuing God as the highest worth leads to a life of loving Him with all our minds, hearts, souls, and strength.

Compare this life to a life centered around worldly possessions. A heroin addict sells his car to get a fix. He loves his heroin. A man gives up his family and friends to advance in his career. He loves his job.

A Christian values God more than anything. His love of God is so strong that no sacrifice is too great, no obedience is too small, to make for Him. The addict gives up heroin. Mother Theresa holds sick babies in her arms. The successful executive leaves it all to offer his skills in a Third World country. A stressed daycare worker takes time to comfort a lonely child.

When God is valued as God, He is more important than

happiness, more precious than any possession, more important than life itself.

Every decision we make, every relationship we have, every word we utter is in some way an expression of our values. Everything we say and do is tied to what we consider to have the greatest and least worth.

Valuing God for himself alone changes the way we pray. Rather than telling God how poor we are and asking for help, we praise Him for how great He is.

If we value God for who He is, we elevate the relationship over the results. Knowing Him and loving Him does not depend on whether He gives us what we want or makes life easy. Even if life is hard, knowing and loving God is still the highest value.

Valuing God for himself alone also revolutionizes worship. Worship is acknowledging the worth of God. When we worship God for himself, we hardly notice who stands at the pulpit; we forget who plays the organ or sings in the choir; we barely think to praise musicians or worship leaders. We are so caught up in loving and praising and worshiping God that everyone else becomes almost invisible and unimportant. Our hearts are filled with God.

"Love the Lord your God with all your heart and with all your soul and with all your mind" . . . He is worth it!

Questions

For Thought:

1. If you knew you only had one month to live, what changes would you make in your daily life? What would become most important to you? What are you doing now that would seem unimportant?
2. If a friend asked you to explain why you believe in God, how would you answer?
3. What takes supreme worth or value in your life?

For Discussion:

1. By valuing things other than God—who is the ultimate value—how do we suffer personally? As a church? As a nation?

2. In what ways do we confuse what God *does* with who He *is*?

3. There are three primary ways for us to gain an understanding of God's supreme value: observation, revelation, and experience. Discuss how we can gain a deeper appreciation of God's value by learning about Him through these means.

4. How can we realign our distorted values with God's eternal, absolute values?

Chapter 4

The Truth,
So Help Me God

WHAT DOES IT SAY about our society when a book entitled *The Day America Told the Truth* becomes a best seller? In this extensively researched volume about Americans' views and values on topics from God to money to intimate relationships we learn that:

- 91% of Americans lie regularly.
- When we refrain from lying, it isn't because we think it is wrong but because we are afraid we will be caught.
- We lie to just about everybody, but the better we know a person the more likely it is that we have told that person a serious lie.
- We lie to get power over other people. We want to control the lives of others.
- We lie because we don't like the way we are and want to shape the impressions of others.
- Two out of three Americans believe that there is nothing wrong with lying. Only 31% of Americans believe that honesty is the best policy.[1]

[1]James Patterson and Peter Kim, *The Day America Told the Truth* (New York: Prentice Hall Press, 1991), 45–49.

All of this, rightly, leads the authors to conclude: "Lying has become a cultural trait of America. Lying is embedded in our national character. . . . Americans lie about everything—and usually for no good reason."[2]

If you think this is an exaggeration, ask yourself whether you would be willing to be hooked up to a lie detector and have those closest to you ask any questions they choose. Or think about how many times you have heard refrains like this (perhaps even in your own mind). . . . *But why tell the truth anyway? . . . If I can lie about a child's age and get a cheaper rate . . . If lying will save my job when jobs are hard to get . . . If someone really doesn't want to hear the truth anyway . . . If it will make me look good. . . . Really, what difference does it make? Especially if it won't hurt anyone.*

Why value truth? The answer is like life . . . a little complex. Let's begin with defining truth.

Truth Is Real and Reliable

The basic characteristic of truth is that it conforms with reality.

When pilots are trained for an instrument rating, one of the significant issues is how to determine truth. When they are flying through a blinding snowstorm and their feelings tell them they are flying upside down, do they go with their feelings or with their instruments? What if their feelings tell them that their instruments are wrong? It is a life or death decision.

At issue is "What is true?" And by true we mean, "Which best conforms with reality?" Therefore, "Which is reliable?"

The same definition applies to mathematics and to courtroom testimony. $2+2=4$ is true because it reflects reality. If you have two oranges on the table and add two more and count the total, you have four oranges. A courtroom testimony about what happened during a bank robbery is judged by the jury to be true or untrue according to how well it fits with reality. True testimony matches the way things really were. True testimony is reliable—you can count on it.

---

[2]Ibid., 49.

Truth about anything can be relied upon. You can plan your future, make your decisions, live your life with truth because it is reliable, dependable, and matches reality.

The Greeks and the Hebrews saw truth in different ways. Greek philosophers thought of truth mostly as statements. You tell the truth. These true words fit with an abstract notion of what is truth. The Hebrews thought of truth more as what a person does—life lived in a way that is dependable, reliable, and consistent with what is real.

Truth is all of this. What a person says is only a part of truth. Truth is also behavior, body language, relationships, promises—it involves all of life.

God Is True Because God Is Always Consistent With Reality

God is "the real thing." Everything He does and everything He says matches with the way everything is. There is nothing fake or counterfeit about God. God is always reliable. You can always count on Him.

The Bible is full of warnings about idols and false gods. You just can't trust them. They are not real, not true.

"You shall have no other gods before me. You shall not make for yourself an idol in the form of anything in heaven above or on the earth beneath or in the waters below" (Exodus 20:3–4).

There is an old philosophic debate about the relationship of God and truth. Some have said that truth is whatever God says it is. If God said that $2+2=5$, then $2+2$ would equal 5. In other words, God determines truth. Other philosophers have argued that truth is greater than God. What makes God so good is that He perfectly conforms with truth as the highest standard of all.

It is beyond our time and purpose to seriously discuss such fine points here, except to say that there is no practical way to divide God and truth. Truth is who God is. Truth is what God does. God and truth are so inseparable that it is ultimately impossible to imagine or to have one without the other.

It's like imagining water without hydrogen or oxygen. If H_2O is what water is, then there is no such thing as water without oxygen—just as there is no such thing as God without truth, or truth without God.

Jesus said, "I am the way and *the truth* and the life" (John 14:6, italics added). God and truth are inseparable.

Truth Is Always Consistent With God

St. Augustine summed it up when he said that "all truth is God's truth." Because God always conforms with reality there is no truth that does not belong to Him. Truth is always consistent with God.

As Christians, then, we never should be afraid that some truth will somehow discredit God or that some archaeological discovery will prove God wrong. What God is and does always fits with reality and truth.

The original concept of "university" was "one truth"— from the Latin words for "one" (uni-) and "truth" (-versity). The student studying astronomy or physics was learning God's truth as much as the student studying philosophy or theology. Unfortunately, many schools that now carry the university title do not adhere to God as the center of truth. Contradictory beliefs and competing claims of truth are taught in the same institution.

These competing claims of truth are no reason for Christians to shy away from learning or to fear new discoveries. To the contrary, whenever and wherever truth is to be found or lived, it will always be 100% compatible with God because that's what truth is.

> Show me your ways, O LORD,
>   teach me your paths;
> guide me in your truth and teach me,
>   for you are God my Savior,
>   and my hope is in you all day long. (Psalm 25:4–5)

I'm sorry to say that the church has not always lived up to this biblical standard. There have been too many times when the church has valued beliefs more than truth.

Galileo discovered the truth that the earth revolves around the sun. He was a believer, a committed Christian, who studied

God's creation to discover the truth about the way it worked. Yet the church condemned him because its own beliefs didn't match with the truth.

What a tragic thing when human beliefs are valued more than God's truth.

Valuing God Means Valuing Truth

Committed Christians always value truth. Or at least we should.

Christians have a long history of active research in science, philosophy, and the arts. It is a strange and inconsistent notion that science and Christianity are somehow contradictory. As long as science seeks the truth, science must be valued by Christians who believe that truth is always consistent with God.

For most of us, however, truth is less a heady search of science and philosophy and more a matter of daily dealing with truthfulness.

Because we value God, we value truth—and valuing truth means hating falsehood. Falsehoods are ungodly. Falsehoods don't match reality. Falsehoods are not reliable. Falsehoods are against God. Falsehoods do damage rather than good. Falsehoods are worthless; they have no value.

The implications continue. Because we value God and truth, we tell the truth. Truth honors God. Truth magnifies God. Truth pleases God. Truth is worth it. Truth has great value because it has God-value.

To understand the practical value of truth, compare it to money. Whenever the world gets into trouble, the value of the U.S. dollar goes up. In quieter times investors feel freer to invest heavily in foreign currencies. But in tumultuous times investors often move to the dollar. Not because green is a more secure color or because our currency is printed on better paper. The value is not in the money itself. The value is in the strength and stability of the United States of America. Over two hundred years of experience has convinced the world's investors that the United States is a country that will stay strong and predictable even when most other countries are plagued with revolution and economic disaster.

In a similar way, the value of truth isn't in the truth alone. Truth gets its value from God, who is reliable, strong, and stable, even when everything else in the universe unravels. Whenever we speak the truth, do the truth, live the truth, we trade and invest in the strength and stability of God himself. Every time we lie or trade in deceit, we are investing our lives in a currency that is as worthless as Monopoly money. We may feel wealthy for the moment, but we will soon discover that the pretend money of untruth has no value in the real world.

The wise author of Proverbs understood all this when he concluded that it is "better to be poor than a liar" (19:22). If someone lies and thereby gets lots of money, he is really poor because money isn't as valuable as truth. It is far better to have a pile of truth and be poor than to have a pile of money and be a liar.

Please don't think this is just a philosophic game playing with words. We are dealing with a basic decision about what we most value in life and why we value it. Truth isn't valuable for itself any more than paper money is valuable for itself. Truth is valuable because it is backed by God just as U.S. dollar bills are valuable because the government of the United States is behind them.

So, then, how do we do it? How do we live truth?

Truth From the Inside

In Psalm 51 the psalmist prays to God: "Surely you desire truth in the inner parts; you teach me wisdom in the inmost place" (51:6).

He rightly understood that God does want us to long for truth on the inside so that we will live the truth on the outside.

Matthew even records a debate Jesus had with the Pharisees about whether evil is what goes into us or what comes out of us. The Pharisees had begun the debate by chastising Jesus because His disciples had broken "the tradition of the elders," not washing their hands before they ate. In wrapping up His conclusions for His disciples, Jesus said:

"But the things that come out of the mouth come from the heart, and these make a man 'unclean.' For out of the heart come evil thoughts, murder, adultery, sexual immorality, theft, false testimony, slander." (Matthew 15:18–19)

Jesus explained that what people put into their mouths is not what makes them bad. Badness comes from inside. People who are bad on the inside will express their evil on the outside.

It is impossible to change a person from the outside in. True change from bad to good can be accomplished only from within. This is not to say that social reform and public laws of righteousness aren't important. They are important because we live in community with one another and need to have positive means to get along together. But never think that laws against murder or rape will make a person good on the inside. The best they can do is restrain a person who is a murderer or rapist on the inside from acting out that internal evil.

Basic to a Christian understanding of humanity and society is the realization that we must be changed as individuals on the inside in order to reform society on the outside. I think the following little parable says it well.

A politician with a preschool son couldn't get his work done because of the boy's constant interruptions and questions. Finally, the father tore a map of the world out of a magazine and cut it up into puzzle-like pieces. He set all the pieces on the table with some plastic tape and told the child to put the world back together again. To the father's surprise, his son returned with the puzzle completed in about five minutes. When he asked how he did it so fast, the little boy explained, "It was easy, Dad. There was a picture of a man on the other side. When I taped the man together, the world came together all by itself."

Because of sin, we start showing our inside selves very young. Some of the earliest manifestations are the lies children tell.

Every parent knows the frustration of dealing with a child who tells a lie—like the mother who was especially frustrated with her two young daughters. When she asked who broke the lamp in the living room, each pointed to the other and said, "She did." Mom said, "One of you is not telling me the truth and I know which one." She said that the liar had a little white pigeon sitting on her shoulder. Instantly, both of them turned to look at the shoulder of the daughter on the right.

Unfortunately, that approach will only work once. Also, in using this ploy Mom lied too, and it wouldn't have taken her daughters long to figure that out.

Parents can sometimes force their children to tell the truth on the outside, but no child will ever grow up to be a truth teller without valuing truth on the inside.

Thousands of sermons have been preached to encourage telling the truth. Most have probably warned against the consequences of lying. There is a crucial difference, however, between telling the truth because we value truth and telling the truth because we are afraid we will be caught if we don't. Ultimately, external warnings and threats will never turn a person who does not value truth from a liar into a truth teller.

Christianity, alone among the world's religions, is not a religion of laws. Laws can only conform a person on the outside; laws never change a person on the inside. Laws are good for establishing and enforcing civil obedience, insuring that—for the most part—people get along with one another. Laws limit misbehavior and make us aware of our inner inadequacies. But laws can never change us on the inside. Even the Ten Commandments can't do that.

Christianity is the message that we must be born again on the inside. When a sinner submits to the person and power of Jesus Christ, there is an internal transformation that alters his or her internal value system.

In computer terminology, we are reprogrammed with entirely new values. We are given God's values. And one of those values is truthfulness.

The only way natural-born liars will ever value and live truth is from the inside out. And if a person consistently lives a lie, that is external evidence that there has been no internal transformation.

If you have a computer or calculator which repeatedly says that $2+12=17$ and that $4\times4=83$, you conclude that there is something wrong inside the computer. It needs a new chip. It should be reprogrammed. So it is with anyone who consistently lies. That person needs to become a Christian.

Becoming a Christian and being programmed to value truth does not change accuracy, but it does change intent. There is a difference. For example, I wear a battery-operated quartz wristwatch. When the battery runs down the watch stops. Sometimes I am unaware when that happens. In an instance like that, if you were to ask me what time it was and I told you it was 9:05 P.M. when it was really 9:25 P.M., I would be inaccurate but I would not be a liar. I intended to tell you the truth. I just had faulty information.

Valuing truth changes our intent, but it does not guarantee our accuracy. However, as Christians we will seek to be accurate. We will always desire to tell the truth even if for some reason we are mistaken.

Truth in Love

Those who value truth must never act as if truth can operate on its own, independent of other values, especially love.

The Bible clearly tells us that we should speak "the truth in love" (Ephesians 4:15). This means that love must always govern the use of truth.

Several years ago I read a heartbreaking letter in Ann Landers's column. It was from a man who had lived with years of guilt over a teenage prank. One evening he and his friends had voted on who was the ugliest girl in their school. Then one of them—the man who had written the letter—called the girl up and congratulated her on being voted the ugliest. Years later, he was still haunted by what he had done.

Technically what he had told that girl was true: the boys did vote and she was chosen. Truth? Maybe. But absolutely lacking in love.

Christians must always use truth lovingly. Truth should help, not hinder, build up, not destroy. Speaking and acting "in love" means that we always act in the best interest of the other person. There may be times, therefore, when the truth is not spoken, when it may be withheld.

There is a difference, however, between loving silence and damaging secrets. Unhealthy relationships are often perpetuated by secrets. For example, many alcoholic families have members who cover up problems by keeping secrets or by outright lying about the addict whom they love. When someone needs help, it is not usually an act of love to keep secrets that keep the help away.

Just as there are such dysfunctional families, there are dysfunctional churches that keep quiet about the sins of leaders as if that were some Christian virtue. The sin that is kept secret festers and grows until many innocent people are injured.

The Bible gives very practical counsel about the relationships of truth, secrets, sins, and confrontation. In Matthew 18:15–17, a formula is presented that begins with a one-on-one conversation. The Christian with the information goes directly to the individual who has sinned and speaks in a way that will help and restore rather than injure or perpetuate. If that doesn't work, the information is carefully shared with another responsible Christian who goes along for a second confrontation with the offender. If that doesn't work, the church or its leadership is brought into the confrontation. Notice that this is a use of truth in a measured, private, and loving manner. Others are not told until and unless absolutely necessary to help the person who needs help. When a positive response is received, there is no need to tell anyone else.

I remember one night when our children were young and our station wagon was packed with neighbor children we were taking home after a weeknight children's club program at church. One of the children started to tell all the others that the parents of one of their friends down the street were getting a divorce. Before he could blurt out the information, my wife kindly interrupted him, saying, "That is Johnny's information to tell." The information was true but it was private. The child whose parents were divorcing could tell his friends when he wanted to tell, but it wasn't another child's information to share. Truth, but private not public.

Whenever such guidelines are presented, someone will always raise new scenarios. The "what ifs" are endless. That is why we must always return to the rule of love. Always ask what is in the best interest of the other person and then do what will help most. Sometimes it will be speaking; sometimes it will be silence. Sometimes it will be very easy; often it will be very hard.

Just remember that truth never stands alone. Truth must always be spoken in love.

Confusing Truth With Importance

While "all truth is God's truth," not all truth is equally important.

Numbers 3:43 says that the total count of Levite males over one month old when Moses was leader of Israel was 22,273.

John 3:16 says that "God so loved the world that he gave his one and only Son, that whoever believes in him shall not perish but have eternal life."

Both of these statements are equally true. But both are not equally important.

Christians, the church, and the world have made enormous mistakes by failing to distinguish levels of importance. We have fought wars, established denominations, and perpetuated family feuds over matters that may have been true but were relatively unimportant.

A usual prerequisite for formal ordination to the ministry of the Gospel is an ordination examination. Different churches use different approaches, although most include a public council where the candidate may be questioned about anything in the Bible, church history, theology, or ministerial practice. In many ways it is comparable to the bar examination for attorneys or board examinations for physicians.

When I was a seminary student, we had frequent classroom discussions about how to answer questions that might be asked on such examinations. One professor suggested that examiners might ask, "Do you consider the doctrine of eschatology to be important?" (Eschatology is the study of "last things" or prophecy of the future based on the Bible.) He then listened while students debated back and forth about the importance of eschatology. When we reached a deadlock, he shared his wisdom. He suggested that we respond to the examiner by asking, "Important for what?" In other words, prophecy may be important as a part of Bible study and interpretation, but it is not important for salvation and eternal life.

Baptism is another example. That which the Bible presents so positively has become a major source of division among many Christians and churches. A friend of mine who had served as a missionary put it in perspective for me with these words: "When they gather up all the Christians and you stand together in front of a firing squad about to die as martyrs for Jesus Christ, mode of baptism is not the topic of discussion."

This is not to suggest that God has multiple and contradictory truths about prophecy or baptism. Nor is this suggesting that these are not important Christian teachings. It is to say that they are not as important as the truth that God exists, that Jesus Christ is God's Son, and that eternal life is gained through faith.

Some truths are unimportant (like the ancient debate over how many angels could sit on the head of a pin). Some truths are important. Some truths are very important. Some truths are extremely important. Some truths are infinitely important.

Family feuds have lasted for generations over differences about truths that really didn't matter. The same can be said about fellowship within the family of God. Some Christians have refused to fellowship with others because of truths as relatively unimportant as the angel count on a pinhead.

We should balance our wholehearted commitment to God's absolute truth with our love for our neighbors as ourselves and our application of God-given wisdom on what is more important and what is less important.

As Christians we want to be true, but we also want to rightly order our priorities. The Bible is enormously helpful in showing what is more and what is less important. God is generous in giving wisdom to those who ask for help in living for the most important.

The Bible begins with the battle for truth in the Garden of Eden. God said, "Don't eat the fruit or you will die." Satan said, "God is wrong." Adam and Eve decided to elevate themselves above God and God's truth. It was a terrible decision and a tragic sin.

Value God. Value the truth. Live the truth. Tell the truth. Speak it in love.

Questions

For Thought:

1. Would you be willing to be hooked up to a lie detector and have those closest to you ask any questions they choose? Why or why not?
2. Would you lie about your child's age to get a discount? Why or why not?
3. How can you get truth in your "inner parts" as David prayed in Psalm 51?
4. Are you living a life of rules and external regulations without an internal transformation? If so, are you willing to submit to the person and power of Jesus Christ, the only One who can transform you and alter your internal value system?

For Discussion:

1. What influences in American society encourage Americans to take lying lightly? How can we counter these influences in the lives of our children?
2. Why is truth dangerous when it operates apart from love? In what ways can it do harm to us and others?
3. What are some of the pitfalls that Christians, the church, and the world can fall into by failing to distinguish levels of importance regarding truth?
4. Discuss the practical counsel about the relationships of truth, secrets, sins, and confrontation that Jesus describes in Matthew 18:15–17. What might be some consequences of not following this advice?

Chapter 5

God's Great Act

THE SUNDAY after the Washington Redskins won the 1992 NFL Super Bowl, Chuck Colson of Prison Fellowship wanted a Redskins player to participate in a service at the Lorton Prison outside of Washington, D.C. Because of the Pro Bowl in Hawaii, none of the players was available, so Head Coach Joe Gibbs volunteered to go instead. It was his first public appearance after winning the Super Bowl.

Gibbs told the inmates about his own brush with the law as a sixteen-year-old when he was driving a car and hit a child riding a bike. Gibbs ran from the accident and was arrested. The child wasn't hurt, but Joe spent the night in jail and faced the wrath of his father, who came to get him. After telling the audience about his encounter with the law, the winning coach talked about Jesus Christ, who was arrested, imprisoned, placed on death row, and executed. He talked about human sin and responsibility for that sin. He told the inmates that real freedom wasn't walking out of jail but committing one's life to Jesus Christ.

Putting everything in biblical perspective, Gibbs told the

prisoners, "If just one of you decides to make that commitment, that would mean, in eternity's value, so much more than the Super Bowl."[1] Many football fans would be amazed that a famous NFL coach values salvation more than a Super Bowl victory.

Red neon signs saying "Jesus Saves" are still flashing in a few places around the country, usually on the front of a skid-row rescue mission or on a rural church building. These electronic bulletins have generated many jokes over the years. Like the one that was supposedly located next to a bank, where some people thought it was advertising that Jesus had a savings account there. Those signs have also, at times, been an embarrassment to some Christians who wonder if the average passersby have any idea what they mean. Or maybe those approaches cheapen something that should be counted as valuable. When TV cameras show a fan in the stands holding a "John 3:16" or "Jesus Saves" sign, it is treated as more of a joke than a joy.

Whatever you think of "Jesus Saves" bumper stickers and signs, did you know that the words themselves are sort of redundant? "Jesus" means "Jehovah is salvation." The line in the Christmas story says, "She [Mary] will give birth to a son, and you are to give him the name Jesus, because he will save his people from their sins" (Matthew 1:21).

Valuing Salvation

There are many reasons Christians highly value salvation, and "once being lost" probably heads the list. Obviously, a person cannot be saved unless he or she was previously lost. Search and Rescue crews don't look for people who are at home watching TV. Lifeguards don't save people sunning on the beach from drowning.

The Bible clearly communicates that every one of us starts out lost: "We all, like sheep, have gone astray, each of us has turned to his own way" (Isaiah 53:6).

---

[1]Chuck Colson, "A Super Bowl Coach Offers a Lesson in Role Modeling," *Urban Family*, Vol. 2, No. 1 (Spring 1993), 16.

In order to be lost, we must be lost from somewhere or someone. The Bible explains that we are all lost from God because of sin. That is both scary and serious.

Think of a time when you were lost and scared. Maybe it was when you were a child on a camping trip. Maybe in the cold and dark of a blizzard. Maybe you think of being lost to bankruptcy or disease.

I think of a day when I borrowed a small boat with an outboard engine to take my wife and baby daughter for a ride on the Intracoastal Waterway and into the harbor of Boca Raton, Florida. Enjoying the beautiful day and the sparkling water, I decided to venture out of the harbor and into the ocean. But the ocean was far rougher than I had anticipated and the waves larger than they had looked from a distance. I realized that we were in a dangerous situation I could not handle and that I needed to head back into the harbor. Then came the horrible realization that I could not see land and I didn't know which way to go. The boat had neither radio nor compass. Just retelling the experience brings back the feelings of lostness—an indescribable mix of helplessness, panic, and desperation.

That day in Florida the potential for tragedy quickly disappeared when I saw other boats and followed them back to safe harbor. At the sight of land my emotions changed from panic to peace, from feeling scared to feeling safe. But I still remember what it was like to be lost, and it helps me value the safety of the shore.

In similar but much greater fashion, Christians value salvation because we know what it was like to be lost from God, lost in sin, lost forever. And once we have been saved from the lostness of sin, we forever value salvation. At least that's the way it should be. But it is easy to take salvation for granted, to become ungrateful. I've tried to figure out why.

Millions of Christians have benefited from growing up in Christian homes, going to church from infancy, and making personal commitments to Christ when they were very young. It is not unusual for these people to say, "I never murdered anyone, robbed a bank, or became sexually promiscuous. I became a Christian as a child and my life hasn't seemed a lot different than it was before." In instances like this there is a temptation, if not a tendency, to barely value salvation at all because there is minimal memory of ever being lost.

I've never met anyone who has had the terrible disease called smallpox. The World Health Organization says that smallpox has been eliminated from earth, except in laboratory vials in the United States and Russia. The only personal experience we have had with smallpox is a childhood inoculation. The only memory is a permanent scar on the arm or leg. Yet smallpox epidemics used to wipe out large populations, spreading quickly and causing painful deaths. On one hand, we should be exceedingly grateful for escaping the deadly disease; on the other hand, it is rather understandable why we take for granted the benefits of this childhood immunization.

To gain a proper perspective, we should ask ourselves, "What would I have been like if I had never become a Christian?" Imagine the loneliness, purposelessness, fear, and sin. Look around at people of similar age whose lives have been a disaster and who have no hope for the future. Taking time to imagine the way we would have been without salvation goes a long way toward understanding this wonderful gift of God and consciously being grateful for it.

Salvation's Cost

One day Jesus saved a lost man named Zacchaeus. When He did, He explained: "Today salvation has come to this house. . . . For the Son of Man came to seek and to save what was lost" (Luke 19:9–10). Zacchaeus, who became one of the most famous tax collectors in history because of his encounter with Jesus, probably didn't fully understand at first. He received God's gift of eternal life. He rode an emotional high from Jesus' impact on him. But not until much later could this man have truly realized that Jesus gave His very life for the life of Zacchaeus.

Jesus, the Son of God, came from heaven for the explicit purpose of saving lost sinners. It wasn't easy. It wasn't cheap. The only way to do it was at the cost of His own life, for as Scripture tells us:

"I lay down my life for the sheep." (John 10:15)

While we were still sinners, Christ died for us. (Romans 5:8)

God made him who had no sin to be sin for us. (2 Corinthians 5:21)

Christ Jesus came into the world to save sinners. (1 Timothy 1:15)

Much more is written in the Bible about the cost of salvation—about how Jesus' death paid the price for our sin in order to save us from eternal lostness and hell. But ultimately, to our finite minds, it is a wonderful mystery far beyond full understanding. What I do know is that I value my salvation because I know it cost Jesus' life.

Carla Ardenghi died on January 25, 1993. She was only twenty-eight years old and she didn't have to die.

Carla was pregnant when she learned that she had cancer. When they discovered the malignancy, the physicians told her they could save her life with chemotherapy or surgery, but she would first have to have an abortion. Carla refused.

When she slipped into a coma, her baby was taken by Caesarean section. He was three months premature and weighed only twenty-three ounces. His mother died eight hours later. She chose to die so that he might live.

When Stefano Ardenghi grows up, do you think he will value his life? I think he will, because of whom it cost.

The same is true for Christians. We value our salvation from lostness and sin and our gift of eternal life . . . because of whom it cost.

Sinners and Saints

Salvation changes us. There is no transformation more profound.

Therefore, if anyone is in Christ, he is a new creation; the old has gone, the new has come. (2 Corinthians 5:17)

But now that you have been set free from sin and have become slaves to God, the benefit you reap leads to holiness, and the result is eternal life. (Romans 6:22)

Neither the sexually immoral nor idolaters nor adulterers nor male prostitutes nor homosexual offenders nor thieves nor the greedy nor drunkards nor slanderers nor swindlers will inherit the kingdom of God. And that is what some of you were. But you were washed, you were sanctified, you were justified in the name of the Lord Jesus Christ and by the Spirit of our God. (1 Corinthians 6:9–11)

Those who have been saved are "being transformed into his [Jesus'] likeness" (2 Corinthians 3:18).

The supernatural benefits of salvation are not only for the distant future in heaven. They are for here and now. God changes us through a supernatural process that makes us look less like lost sinners and more like Jesus Christ.

Some Christians don't see this and, therefore, don't fully value salvation. Keenly aware of our own sinfulness and woeful shortcomings, we tend to focus on what still needs changing rather than rejoicing over what has already been changed. For those who struggle with this look-what's-still-wrong-with-us worry, here are two principles to consider:

#1: "Being transformed" is a lifelong process; it doesn't happen all at once. It's somewhat like restoring a wrecked and rusty old car into mint condition. It takes a lot of time and work. The good news is that God promises to completely restore everyone He saves.

#2: Don't just compare the way you are now to the way you're going to be someday. Also compare the way you are now to the way you would have been if you weren't saved. When you do this, you begin to realize the supernatural difference God has already made in your life.

I get impatient that I'm not more like Jesus. There's so much in me that still needs to be changed. I have a long way to go. But then I think about what I would be like if God had not saved me. My life would be a wreck. Sin would have taken over. I hate to think about it. God has made a great difference in my life, and that is just one of the reasons I value salvation.

A Matter of Life and Death

Last, but certainly not least, Christians value salvation because it changes our eternal destiny. We are saved from hell to heaven, from death to life, from the eternal consequences of sin to the eternal pleasures of God.

> Whoever believes in the Son has eternal life, but whoever rejects the Son will not see life, for God's wrath remains on him. (John 3:36)
> [Jesus said:] "I give them eternal life, and they shall never perish; no one can snatch them out of my hand." (John 10:28)

If you were to die today, do you know for sure that you would go to heaven?

Anyone who is a Christian—anyone who has been saved—can know without a doubt. God says so. God promises. That's valuable beyond description or price.

I try to imagine living without this assurance. I would be afraid to drive down the highway for fear I would be hit and killed, not knowing if I would go to heaven. I would be afraid to have medical treatments. I would want to stay home all the time—but even if I did that, I couldn't go to sleep because the house might catch on fire and the fire consume me.

An enormous value of salvation is the freedom to live without this kind of constant fear. With salvation comes the assurance of God that death is not disaster. On the other side of death is guaranteed eternal life in heaven with God. No wonder Christians value salvation.

Having lots of reasons to value salvation isn't enough, however; if we really value salvation, we won't be able to hide it.

Responses to Salvation

Do you ever watch the responses of the TV game show guests when they win the big prizes? They go wild with gratitude. They jump up and down. They kiss and hug the host. They say, "Thank you! Thank you! Thank you!" All because they've won $25,000 or a new car or a trip to Hawaii or something else that won't last very long.

Gratitude is always the first and most appropriate response when we get something very good.

Several years ago my brother Paul stopped by the side of the road to help a woman who had been in an accident. No one else had bothered to stop. She not only thanked him then, but sent him a gift. And she still calls and sends gifts every year in gratitude for his help.

Since salvation is the best gift we can ever get—the best thing that can ever happen to us—it should lead us to the wildest gratitude possible. We should thank God a million times. Thank Him every day. Give Him gifts. Sing. Shout. Praise.

It is unimaginable that someone rescued from a burning building would not thank the fire fighter who saved his or her life. It should be equally unimaginable for any Christian saved from sin and eternal death not to want to thank God. Not because we have to, but because we want to. We welcome the opportunity. It is our delight.

> And we pray this in order that you may live a life worthy of the Lord and may please him in every way ... giving thanks to the Father, who has qualified you to share in the inheritance of the saints in the kingdom of light. For he has rescued us from the dominion of darkness and brought us into the kingdom of the Son he loves, in whom we have redemption, the forgiveness of sins. (Colossians 1:10, 12–14)
>
> Thanks be to God for his indescribable gift! (2 Corinthians 9:15)

The second response to the value of salvation is *faith*. Faith is the means by which we receive salvation. God does the work, giving what is needed to save us. Our responsibility is to believe Him and receive it.

Faith always has an object: We must have faith *in* something or someone, which means we trust that person or thing. We trust that a bridge will hold us up when we drive across it; we trust the bank when we deposit our money there.

Think of it in terms of someone drowning out in the North Atlantic. The Coast Guard sends a rescue helicopter, and a diver comes down on a rope, reaches out, and yells, "Take my hand!" What does the drowning man do? Does he ask to see a certificate assuring him the helicopter is airworthy? Does he ask to see the credentials of the diver? No, he grabs the diver's hand, trusting that the diver will save him.

Faith is like grabbing the hand of God. Faith is taking Him at His word. Faith is believing Him. It's the only way to be saved. Good deeds never saved anyone. Neither did baptism nor church membership nor growing up in a nice family. As the Bible says, "It is by grace you have been saved, through faith" (Ephesians 2:8).

Bottom line? It works! Have faith in God for salvation and you are saved.

Since we are saved by faith, we should also live by faith. Certainly if we can trust God to save us from sin and guarantee heaven, we can trust Him with our jobs, our families, and our health—or anything else.

Nothing is as important as our souls, and no time is as long as forever. This is the whole idea behind the simple declaration in Romans: "The righteous will live by faith" (Romans 1:17). It's just a perfectly logical response to the value of salvation: Live by faith. Put your hand in the hand of God and trust Him for whatever is the issue or crisis of life right now.

Faith is what the saved life is all about. No wonder, then, that the word "faith" appears over three hundred times in the New Testament alone. It's the way to go.

A third response to the value of salvation is our *lifestyle*, for it only makes sense that the way we live should reflect what has happened to us. . . . We've been saved!

The movie *The Doctor* is based on the true story of a surgeon who was arrogant and insensitive—until he himself got cancer and became the patient. From that vantage point, he began to see everything differently. Fortunately his cancer was cured and he returned to the practice of medicine, but he was a very different man and doctor because of what had happened to him. His own malignancy, surgery, and recovery transformed his lifestyle. He had a new sensitivity toward patients. He now treated others with respect, and the pain and fear of his patients connected with his own emotions. The differences were so marked that his colleagues were amazed.

And whatever you do, whether in word or deed, do it
all in the name of the Lord Jesus, giving thanks to God the
Father through him. (Colossians 3:17)

But the fruit of the Spirit is love, joy, peace, patience,
kindness, goodness, faithfulness, gentleness and self-con-
trol. Against such things there is no law. Those who belong
to Christ Jesus have crucified the sinful nature with its pas-
sions and desires. Since we live by the Spirit, let us keep in
step with the Spirit. (Galatians 5:22–25)

In other words, anyone saved from sin who really values salvation will adopt a lifestyle for the Savior and against the sin.
Unfortunately this has sometimes become a source of tension
and misunderstanding between Christians.

Individuals who have been saved from sin often hate their
old lifestyles as much as ex-smokers hate cigarettes, and they
adopt their new lifestyle with a passionate enthusiasm to live
differently from the past and wholeheartedly for God. The
problem is not with the transformation or the enthusiasm. The
problem comes when the new lifestyle is imposed on others who
have not shared the same spiritual experience.

The old lifestyle may have included drunkenness, laziness,
and stinginess. The new lifestyle is just the opposite—a life of
abstinence, disciplined hard work, and great generosity. That is
all wonderful and appropriate. However, it becomes legalism
when this new lifestyle is forced upon others as a legal code.

The tragedy is not so much the legalism as the way it dis-
tracts from the transformation of salvation. It is like ignoring the
birth of a baby and giving all the attention to the birth certificate. If there is no baby, the birth certificate is meaningless.

Christian values should always return the worth to what is
most important. Lifestyle change is a necessary response and a
proof of salvation, but the far greater value is in the salvation.

A fourth response to the value of salvation is *witness*—telling
someone else.

Think of it this way: If you had a painful disease with obvious symptoms and no known cure, you'd be thrilled if you
found a physician who cured you and saved your life. What if
you then met a neighbor or even saw a stranger with the same
disease? Wouldn't you want to tell that person how his or her

life could also be saved? Or would you say, "Sickness and doctors are very private. Two things I never talk about are politics
and where to be cured of a terminal illness"? Hardly!

Well, our witness to our salvation is the same thing. We must
tell everyone who needs what we needed. Send everyone possible to the Great Physician who cures and saves the soul.

Jesus commands all Christians to be witnesses:

> "But you will receive power when the Holy Spirit comes
> on you; and you will be my witnesses in Jerusalem, and in
> all Judea and Samaria, and to the ends of the earth." (Acts
> 1:8)
> We are therefore Christ's ambassadors, as though God
> were making his appeal through us. (2 Corinthians 5:20)

The most important questions anyone can ever be asked are
"Have you been saved? Do you have God's salvation from sin
to eternal life?"

If the answer is yes, value your salvation. If the answer is no,
receive His salvation. Pray to God and tell Him that in faith you
want to receive His gift of eternal life through Jesus Christ.

Questions

For Thought:

1. Can you recall a time as a child when you were lost—in a
   storm, at sea, in a forest? How did you feel? If you are a
   Christian, imagine what your life would be like now if you
   had never experienced the salvation of God. How do you
   think your life would be different?
2. Think of one situation or crisis you are facing right now and
   tell God that you are putting your *faith* in Him to see you
   through it.
3. Ask God to show you any aspects of your present *lifestyle*

that do not yet reflect the inner changes God has worked in you. In faith commit those areas to Him, trusting Him to work the outward changes into your life.

4. Consider how you could become a more effective *witness* for Jesus Christ. Ask God to help you be more sensitive to the promptings of His Spirit as you encounter people who need to hear of God's salvation.

For Discussion:

1. The Bible categorically states that "we all, like sheep, have gone astray, each of us has turned to his own way" (Isaiah 53:6). To be *lost* we must be lost from somewhere or some-one. Discuss what being lost from God means.

2. Take time to discuss the incredible cost it took God, our Father, to get salvation for us.

3. The apostle Paul says in 2 Corinthians 3:18 that we "are being transformed into his [Jesus'] likeness." How is that practically worked out in our daily lives?

4. Gratitude, faith, lifestyle, and witness are four correct responses to the great gift of salvation. Discuss how each response can be strengthened in our lives.

Chapter 6

Being Like God

TRUE OR FALSE: "Cleanliness is next to godliness."

Answer: "If the Bible says it, it must be true!"

Whether it is true or not, it's not from the Bible. The quote comes from a sermon by John Wesley, founder of the Methodist church. It's interesting, though, that while just about everyone knows what cleanliness is—even to the extent of thinking it is commanded in the Bible—few have a clear idea of what godliness is.

It says in 1 Timothy 4:8 that "godliness has value for all things, holding promise for both the present life and the life to come."

Godliness is an important value for everything in this life and the next life. Godliness is the Christian's description for living and dying, working and playing, thinking and reading, traveling and staying home, saving and spending, getting married, raising children, praying and sleeping.

If that's correct, godliness is the great unknown dream that most of humanity is looking for. What else has a value that lasts beyond this life and into eternity? Certainly not our houses and businesses. A million-dollar house or a billion-dollar business is worthless in terms of the life to come. Possibly the epitome of this is the ancient Egyptian monarchs who were buried in their huge pyramid tombs, surrounded by their most valued possessions, their furniture, food, and even buried-alive servants. As valuable as those assets were in this life, not even a Pharaoh could take them with him when he died.

But, in contrast, godliness is valuable now and we can take it with us.

Godliness Is Devotion to God

The New Testament was written in Greek, and the Greek word for "godliness" is *eusebeia*. The word originally meant "to step back" or "to keep a distance" and was used in relation to worship of the Greek gods in ancient temples. If the Greeks had a right attitude toward their gods, they would "step back" and "keep a distance" away from them.

By the time the New Testament was written, the word had come to mean "a right attitude" toward the gods. Or, as we would say, "devotion." If you are devoted to another person, you have a right attitude of respect and allegiance.

Godliness, then, is devotion to God. Often, however, people think of godliness as behavior when it is really an attitude. This zeroes in on the central core of Christianity.

Christianity is not an outside-in religion; it is an inside-out relationship with God. Whether considering the practices of the Hebrews in the Old Testament or Christians since the New Testament, the rituals are not most important. Those who perform the liturgy, offer sacrifices, and conform to the rules are not necessarily godly. Likewise, it is possible to have a right attitude of devotion to God and mess up the liturgies and rituals and rules. David is the classic example. He ate the consecrated bread in the Tabernacle reserved exclusively for the priests. Even beyond that, he committed adultery with Bathsheba and ordered the murder of her husband Uriah. Yet after all that, David is described as a man after God's heart. His external behavior was at times ungodly but he still had a heart devoted to God.

The eventual problem with this understanding of godliness

is obvious. The most blatant of sinners can argue, "I may be awful on the outside but I sure do love God on the inside." This is absurd. There is an essential link between attitude and actions. David's core attitude of devotion to God brought him to great sorrow and repentance. Outward sin is never acceptable. However, the priority of attitude over action cannot be escaped. It is fundamental to Christian teaching.

Life Centered on God

Everybody has a center of life. The center of our life is what is most important to us. It is what controls everything else about us.

Some lives are centered on music or medicine or money. Some lives are centered on work, some on play. Some parents' lives are centered on their children, and every important decision is based on what is best for their sons and daughters. They sacrifice their own interests and well-being for their children. They dream about good for their children and they dread any bad in their children's lives. I know a woman in her seventies who is chronically ill because of her anxiety over her son who is now in his forties. She always mentions him in conversations. He lives a life of repeated disasters, often taking full advantage of his mother's sympathy. Her life revolves around her "boy."

The most common center of life is self. This is a natural human inclination. We tend to think of ourselves as more important than others. We are concerned about how we look, the way others treat us, and what our rights are. Depression and anger often result from this self-centeredness, for life is not always the way we want it to be.

This inclination toward self-centeredness has dramatically escalated during the last half of the twentieth century. Today, we are a generation devoted to ourselves. This is evidenced by the growth of the psychotherapy and counseling industry, the popularity of the recovery movement, and the millions of self-help books sold. Our vocabulary brims with "self" words such as self-esteem, self-worth, and self-talk, and *Self* magazine has a wide circulation.

This self-centeredness has also shown up in the Christian

community. If you doubt this, just consider the interpretation this generation has given to Jesus' Great Commandment: " 'Love the Lord your God with all your heart and with all your soul and with all your mind'. . . . [and] 'Love your neighbor as yourself' " (Matthew 22:37–39). We have turned this teaching into a promotion of self-love, saying that "unless we first learn to love ourselves, we will never be able to obey Jesus and love others as ourselves."

Now, don't get me wrong—there can be great value in many of these self emphases. I've often taught the concepts myself, explaining the necessity of self-love in order to love others. But I also must admit that the ballooning of some of these good concepts has too often bloated to the point of disgust. Good things taken to an extreme can become very bad. It is bad when Christians adopt self-centeredness instead of God-centeredness as the fulcrum of life.

When you were a child, did you ever work with a small magnet and metal shavings in a home science kit or a science experiment at school? I remember spreading bits of metal over a piece of paper and then running a small magnet along the underside of the paper. All of the metal bits quickly moved across the paper and lined up in relationship to the magnet. If I moved the magnet, the bits of metal moved. All the pieces centered around the unseen magnet.

That's the way Christians live when we value godliness. All the pieces of our lives—job, health, relationships, time, income, sex, recreation, family, even thoughts—line up in relation to the God we do not see. He is the magnetic center of our lives. The pull of God is stronger than anything else. Life is centered on Him.

Remember, godliness is an attitude and a value. It is the deep, motivating belief that a God-centered life is worth much more than a self-centered life.

Life Committed to God

Devotion to God is not only the central magnetic pull to God, it is also our commitment. Christians are convinced that God is great and good. It's not that God is overpowering us and we are being dragged along, kicking and screaming against His pull. We want our lives centered on Him; we enjoy having our lives centered on Him. We are committed to God.

You might compare this to a soldier during wartime. When the United States entered World War I and World War II, the government drafted young men to fight. On the one hand, it could be argued that those soldiers were on the front lines because the government was like a giant magnet pulling them there. They had no choice. It was almost impossible to resist. But the records from the past and the testimonials of survivors report that they wanted to be there. They were fiercely patriotic and welcomed military service. They were even willing to die for their country. To these veterans "patriotism" is one of the most wonderful and emotional words in their vocabulary. They believed wholeheartedly in the cause and the country. They were committed.

That's the way it is with Christians who value godliness. Our lives are centered on God and we are committed to Him. We would die for Him because we believe God is worth our lives. It's far more than submitting to the power of God, although it is that. Godliness is like patriotism only more so—an enthusiastic and wholehearted allegiance to God. Committed Christians are convinced nothing else really matters or lasts. God is the only permanent value to be committed to. "Since everything will be destroyed in this way, what kind of people ought you to be? You ought to live holy and godly lives . . ." (2 Peter 3:11).

We could also compare this to investments. If you were convinced that every other investment would fail except gold, you would commit everything you had to gold. Christians who value godliness are convinced that God is the only investment that will last, so we commit everything we have to Him. We are fully invested in God.

It isn't always easy. "In fact, everyone who wants to live a godly life in Christ Jesus will be persecuted" (2 Timothy 3:12). It seems strange to us that Christians in the early centuries of the church seemed to take pride in the persecution they received. When they suffered abuse and torture, imprisonment and even death, they often expressed delight. But their delight wasn't in the problems or the pain. Their delight was in what the persecution proved—and that was their commitment to Jesus Christ. They reasoned that only the truly committed were persecuted, and they valued godly commitment far more than personal comfort.

I was in Dallas shortly after the Cowboys won the 1993 Super Bowl, and you can never guess what everyone seemed to be talking about. Signs and headlines and pennants were everywhere. Downtown, I overheard three men discussing Cowboy Coach Jimmy Johnson. "Jimmy Johnson lives football. . . . Nothing else matters to the man. It's all he talks about. . . . He sees everything in terms of football. . . . Jimmy Johnson is devoted to football." You could say that Coach Johnson has "footballness." That's what he values.

Christians value God. We are devoted to God. We want our life centered on God, committed to God. You can call what we've got "godliness." We see everything in terms of that commitment: jobs, marriage, family, personal relationships—everything. We should not be surprised when others talk behind the committed Christian's back and say, "All that guy ever thinks about is God!"

Devotion to God leads to the other side of godliness, which is living like God.

Life Lived Like God

Some people have trouble making sense out of what it means to "live like God." That religious terminology doesn't quite fit with our modern world. It sounds too abstract. Yet we commonly hear about someone who "lives like hell." That's religious terminology, too, and we all know what it means.

So living like hell is hellishness. The opposite is living like God, and that is godliness. But what does this mean in practical terms?

One of the best lines in the Bible to help us understand what it means to live like God comes from Philippians 2:5: "Your attitude should be the same as that of Christ Jesus." In other words, Christians must understand and value the attitude of Jesus.

What was Jesus like when He lived on earth? His attitude is

described as an attitude of humility and servanthood.

When we get to know others well, we usually have a pretty good idea what their attitudes are about most things. So the more we learn about Jesus and the better we get to know Him, the easier it will be to figure out what His attitude would be.

For example, what do you think Jesus' attitude would be toward children? Money? Getting a promotion? Getting fired? What would His attitude be if somebody were angry at Him? Disagreeing with Him? Doing something stupid? Being lazy? What would His attitude be toward prayer? Divorce? Fishing? And the list goes on and on. (By the way, Jesus had a really positive attitude toward fishing!)

We need to have those same responses as Jesus. Picture Jesus in the situation you are in. Then remember your attitude should match that of Christ Jesus. That is godliness: having an attitude like Jesus.

Attitudes produce actions. Even though godliness does not begin with actions, it normally results in actions as we live it out. We all face situations every day where we must choose how to behave. The question is: "What would God do?"

Would God blow up and lose His cool?

Would God lie?

Would God forgive?

Would God be kind and generous?

When I was growing up, some adults in our church used an approach like this to impose certain social behavior on us teenagers. They would ask us if we could imagine Jesus attending the theater, going to a dance, or hanging out in a bar. Of course, the implication was that we should stay away from such places if we wanted to be like Jesus. I remember thinking at the time that I couldn't imagine Jesus eating pizza, driving a Mustang, or going to the bathroom. Did that mean I should abstain from such activities? The basic question is good but capable of being ridiculously misapplied.

In fact, Jesus did hang out with people at places for which He was severely criticized. Legalists of His day called Him a drunkard, a glutton, and a friend of sinners. Sometimes those who are really like Jesus may be the very persons condemned for their social friendships and activities.

Godliness is not isolation or escape from society and culture. To the contrary, godliness forces us to penetrate the culture as Jesus did in the Incarnation. But Jesus did this without sinning. He never sinned. His attitude was right in every situation.

Christians have spent twenty centuries bouncing back and forth between legalism and license. What this has proved above all, perhaps, is that we cannot define godliness with a set of rules and we cannot live without discipline. We tend toward either legalism or license because that is the easy way to deal with hard circumstances. It is always easier to have a rule to refer to, or else to just behave lawlessly. It is a far harder approach to know God well and analyze each situation and relationship in terms of His person and character—and then act out of a godly attitude and in accord with God's values.

Still, even then, we don't always get it right. We misjudge and misbehave. We are often inconsistent. But godliness is not perfection. It is an attitude of heart, mind, and soul—loving God and attempting to be like Him.

Imagine yourself, in a small way, in God's situation. There He is, extremely busy running the universe, dealing with some wonderful people and some terrible people. Some of His children have turned out great but many have broken His heart. He regularly encounters birth and death, good and bad, marriage and divorce, angels and demons, riches and poverty, pleasure and pain.

God faces everything. And so do we. In our own finite way we have daily opportunities to view things from God's perspective, to act like God when great joys come and when horrors hit, when our plans come together and when they are thwarted, when people love us and when people hate us, when the votes are for us and when the votes are against us. Life is an ongoing opportunity to live godliness—to act like God.

Whatever we are now facing or will someday face, the big deal is not what is happening but whether we handle what happens with the attitudes and actions of God himself.

Big question: "Do I have what it takes to be godly? Is it really possible to think and act like God?"

Consider this: "[God's] divine power has given us everything we need for life and godliness through our knowledge of him who called us by his own glory and goodness" (2 Peter 1:3). In other words, God guarantees to give us whatever it takes to be godly.

Do you remember the popular song "The Wind Beneath My Wings" about flying higher than an eagle because a friend is like the wind that lifts the eagle's wings? Well, Christians who value godliness have their own eagle's wings: "Those who hope in the LORD will renew their strength. They will soar on wings like eagles; they will run and not grow weary, they will walk and not be faint" (Isaiah 40:31).

Those are the words of God to Christians who value godliness. We can respond that God is our hero; He is everything we would like to be. We can fly higher than eagles because God is the wind beneath our wings.

Questions

For Thought:

1. Godliness in the New Testament is centered around devotion to God. How can you strengthen your attitude of respect and allegiance to Jesus Christ?
2. Think of parts of your life in which you are more concerned with the "outside rituals" of Christianity than the "inner issues" of the heart.
3. Why is God the only permanent value to be committed to?
4. Think about what your life is centered on: God, your children, your work, your money, yourself? Ask God to reveal to you what He thinks you focus most of your attention on.

For Discussion:

1. Why is godliness an important value for everything in this life and the next life?

2. According to the New Testament, is "godliness" a behavior or an attitude?

3. In this generation we have misconstrued the meaning of Jesus' command to love others *as we love ourselves* by over-emphasizing the need for self-love before we can truly love others. Do you agree or disagree? What do *you* think Jesus meant by that command?

4. We can't live like God simply by following a list of rules. Instead, we need to know Him so well that we can figure out how *He* would respond in any given circumstance and act as He would. Do you think it's possible to know God in this way? How can we get to know God?

Chapter 7

Believing Is Seeing

HER HUSBAND had left her. He said he didn't love her any-more. There was someone else. I could see the hurt in her eyes. She had every right to be devastated and angry, yet she was filled with optimism.

"He's going to come back to me. He won't divorce me. And our relationship will be better than before." She had no interest in attending a divorce recovery workshop, she told me. Instead, she joined a support group of men and women whose spouses had left them but who were convinced that their marriages would be restored. They gathered to pray together and claim Bible promises about marriage restoration.

"How can you be so sure your marriage will be restored?" I asked her. She explained that she had faith.

Their divorce was finalized. She still insisted that he would come back to her. She said that when they were remarried their relationship would become the best that it would ever be. She said that she was absolutely convinced because she had faith.

Then, although he'd had no previous health problems and

was only in his forties, her former husband unexpectedly died. And they never reconciled. . . .

A couple came to talk to me about a problem. I knew their child was desperately ill and I assumed that was the topic. They talked about their love for their son and about how hard it was to see him suffer. Then they told me about another problem that significantly added to their pain.

Several people had called them, telling of nontraditional medical remedies that were sure to cure. Another person had given pointed religious advice: "Your son will be healed if you have enough faith. Have faith and he will get better. It's not up to doctors, it's up to you. If you don't have faith, your son will die."

These parents loved their son and desperately wanted him to recover. And though they loved God and believed He had the power to heal, they did not feel they had the kind of faith that was being demanded of them. They were struggling with a sense of guilt that their son would die because of their shortage of faith. They wanted to know if God really operates that way, killing children because their parents don't have enough faith.

Their son did not die. He recovered. . . .

Then there was the hardened professor's response when one of his students used the word "faith" in his classroom. "Faith is a crutch for the weak," he stated. "Faith is fantasy. It's wishful thinking. It makes no difference at all." He belittled the Christian students whom he quickly identified as if he were on some kind of witch hunt. He wrote cruel comments on any papers that reflected religious belief and seemed to take perverse satisfaction out of humiliating anyone who did not affirm his atheism.

Compare these true stories with what the Bible says:

> We live by faith, not by sight. (2 Corinthians 5:7)
> The only thing that counts is faith expressing itself through love. (Galatians 5:6)
> "If you have faith as small as a mustard seed, you can say to this mountain, 'Move from here to there' and it will move. Nothing will be impossible for you." (Matthew 17:20)

Everything that does not come from faith is sin. (Romans 14:23)

When it comes to the meaning of faith, people run the gamut from strange to stupid to skeptical to sincere to scriptural. Our popular culture is loaded with references to faith. We talk about "blind faith," "faith healers," and deposits secured by the "full faith" of the United States government.

Faith is trust. Faith is believing in someone or something. I have faith in my wife. I trust her. I have faith in the highway bridge near my house. I trust it. Faith is believing that someone or something will do what they are supposed to do.

When Charleen and I were married, she promised that she would take me for better or for worse, for richer or for poorer, in sickness and in health, and cling to me and to me alone, so long as we both shall live. I trust her to do all of that—what she promised and is expected to do as my wife.

The bridge is different. I don't expect the bridge to cling to me and to me alone so long as we both shall live. I just expect it to hold my car as I drive from one side to the other. That's what it is supposed to do.

I value faith. It would be impossible to live without it. If I didn't trust my wife, the bridge, doctors, money, or the water supply, life would be impossible.

The same goes for God. I trust Him. I have faith in Him. I am convinced that God will do what He is supposed to do— what He has promised to do—as God.

I especially value faith in God, because the things I trust Him for are far more important than anything else. I value faith in God because God will stick with me even if my marriage fails, the bridge collapses, the doctor goofs, or the currency becomes worthless.

I value faith in general because I couldn't live without it.

I value faith in God because I couldn't live now and I couldn't live forever without Him.

The Basis for Faith's Value

Too often people make faith into something it is not. In a sense they overvalue it. Let me explain.

The value of faith is never in faith itself. This seems so obvious, yet many make this mistake. They really believe that they can make something happen because of the power of their faith. But faith by itself is nothing. Faith on its own doesn't make anything happen.

I remember one time when we were living in Colorado and Charleen's parents had come for a visit. I can't recall the context, but I made a passing comment that something bad might happen. My mother-in-law said, "Don't say that. It might happen." (I'm not proud of the way I responded, but for purposes of illustration, I'll continue with the incident.) Later Charleen and I took them sightseeing in the mountains, and as we drove up a steep road I said, "Those rocks could fall down and crush the car." ("Don't say that. It might happen," came the reply.) As we went around a bend I said, "The front tire could blow out and we could go over the side and drop 2,000 feet." ("Don't say that. It might happen.") When we came back down the mountain I said, "The brakes might overheat and we won't be able to stop going down this road." ("Don't say that. It might happen.")

None of these bad things happened, because my saying so doesn't make bad things happen. Likewise, having faith or even saying so doesn't make good things happen. The value of faith is not in faith itself. The value of faith comes from its object.

Faith is like the electrical cord that comes with an appliance. The cord is the means to connect to the power that makes the appliance work. If you plug the cord into your ear, the refrigerator will not cool and the toaster will not toast. But if you plug the cord into an electrical outlet connected to a source of power, powerful things can happen.

Too many people have faith in the wrong object; they have faith in faith, in themselves, in their financial security, in their government. All of these can fail. The most valuable faith is faith in God, because it connects us to the greatest power in the universe.

Steps of Faith

There is a simple progression in the practical recipe of faith; it begins with conviction, moves to commitment, and results in response.

First is the conviction that God is God and that He can do what He says He can do. When God says that He can give us peace in the middle of life's hurricanes, power to deal with evil, and salvation from hell, true faith says, "I am convinced that's true. God can do anything."

Conviction is not enough, however. According to James 2:19, even the demons are convinced God is God and shudder at the thought of Him. But they're not committed. For faith to do what it is supposed to do, it must move from conviction to commitment.

A long time ago I was convinced that WalMart was a good stock to buy. I read a lot of articles about it long before the company opened a store anywhere close to my home. Later, WalMart stock soared and the company became the largest retailer in the United States—although I never bought a single share of WalMart stock. I was right in my conviction but I never committed. Commitment would have moved me from a general acknowledgment of WalMart's worth to a serious plan to invest.

Christian faith must move beyond conviction *about* God to commitment *to* Him. Faith is investing everything a person is and has with God.

Faith that begins with conviction and moves to commitment results in response. That is, doing something about it. Action. Living accordingly. It's marrying the person, driving across the bridge, buying the stock, doing what God says.

Some may say, "I don't get all these distinctions. To me it's all one thing. Faith is believing in God, committing to God, responding to God. It's all the same." Good enough! Because they are all wrapped up together.

Important Questions About Faith

Actually, faith is one of the most controversial and puzzling aspects of Christianity and frequently leads to certain questions.

Question #1: Is faith really important?

According to Hebrews 11:6 it is: "And without faith it is impossible to please God, because anyone who comes to him must believe that he exists and that he rewards those who earnestly seek him."

As far as a relationship with God is concerned, faith is Number One in importance. It is the *only* way for a person to connect to God.

Question #2: If I have faith, can I get what I want?

Maybe.

If you have faith, you can get what you want if that's the same as what God wants and said He would do.

Many people think they can get rich, be cured of cancer, or change another person's behavior if they have enough faith. That may be like plugging a refrigerator into an electrical outlet and expecting it to wash your clothes.

Remember—faith is believing something will do what it is supposed to do. God never promised He would make every Christian rich or healthy or solve all our problems. God is not a genie in some Aladdin's lamp that is rubbed with faith and made to do whatever we please.

Faith is believing and acting on God's promises, which range from grace sufficient to face any problem to peace through any stress. God has given us a Book full of supernatural promises. Faith is our way to plug into those promises and see them come true in our experience.

Question #3: What about the healings and miracles in the Bible that are connected with faith? How did that work?

Indeed they were connected with faith. Just as healings and miracles are connected to faith today.

Faith is asking God to do what He promises and trusting Him to do it. But God does not promise routine miracles or guarantee routine healings. He does, however, promise to provide what is best, to meet our needs, to show His power, and to make everything work together for good. He consistently does all of these things, but He does them in different ways for different people in different instances. Faith is believing He keeps His word through multiple means. Sometimes that has involved healings or miracles. At other times it has not.

Christians in seemingly similar circumstances have extremely contrasting experiences. Some trust God and are healed; some trust God and suffer and die. Which do you think takes greater faith—seeing the power and love of God in miraculous healing or seeing the power and love of God in miserable suffering? I believe that both take great faith.

Question #4: Do some people have more faith than others?

Yes, they do. It is difficult to understand this, but the Bible teaches that God gives the spiritual gift of special faith to some but not all (1 Corinthians 12:9).

Think of it this way. Have you bought an extension cord lately? I had to shop for one last December after someone ran over our fifty-foot electrical cord to the outdoor Christmas lights with a snowblower. At the local discount store I found plenty to choose from. Some were long. Some were short. Some were for indoors and some were for outdoors. Some could carry a lot more electricity a lot farther than others. But every one was designed to connect to a lot of power—at least 110 volts of it.

In much the same way, we are varied in our faith. Some of us are designed for more and others are designed for less. Some are for short distances and others are for very long distances. Some of us have to have faith for one circumstance, some for another. No matter which describes us, most of us have never carried a fraction of the faith that God designed us to carry. But every one of us is able to connect directly to God. And God is infinitely more powerful than 110 volts.

Let us worry less about how our faith compares to someone else's and focus on the stunning privilege of living by faith—plugged into God, believing God, getting our power for life from God.

Question #5: What is an example of living by faith?

Ephesians 6:12 reveals that "our struggle is not against flesh and blood, but against the rulers, against the authorities, against the powers of this dark world and against the spiritual forces of evil in the heavenly realms."

Do you believe that? Do you believe that your present struggles in life are mostly a spiritual war against Satan and evil and not primarily a struggle with your boss or a family member? That's what God's Word says. It takes faith to believe that because it's hard to prove. If it's true, our only chance of winning in life is to hook up to the power of God and expect Him to supernaturally beat off evil and bring good. If it's not true, we're crazy to pray and lazy to expect God to solve our problems.

Another example. You need a job. Or you are sick. Or you are worried sick about your son's drug use. You've done everything you know to do about the situation—so it's not that you've been irresponsible. But there is nothing more that you can do. Will you trust God to handle the situation and believe that He is doing what is right regardless of how it comes out? That's faith. It's trusting God and being convinced that whatever He does will be good and right.

Remember, our faith is in God, not in the process or the outcome. Philippians 1:29 gives another hard example: "For it has been granted to you on behalf of Christ not only to believe on him, but also to suffer for him." We do not seek or choose suffering, and many of us don't suffer a great deal. However, the test of our concept of faith is clearer in a negative experience. If our definition of faith only works for experiences that are easy and pleasant, we have an inadequate understanding of faith.

Not all examples of faith are tough. In most of life, in fact, many of the examples are very pleasant, for "every good and perfect gift is from above, coming down from the Father" (James 1:17).

God is good and generous; His gifts are fantastic. He just pours it on and on. But we shouldn't value faith for the good we can get. Value faith for the God it connects us to.

Those who value faith look for every opportunity to trust God. When the bills come. In school. On a first date. When laid off. At the hospital. While meeting an old friend. Every situation in life—whether good or bad—is a great new opportunity to trust God, connect to God, plug into God, do it for God. Faith is seeing and experiencing God in everything.

Recently the Minnesota Department of Transportation launched a campaign to reduce accidents involving cars and motorcycles. Whenever cars collide with motorcycles, the driver of the motorcycle is almost always injured more severely than the driver of the car. And the driver of the car almost always says, "I didn't see the motorcycle!" This scenario has happened so frequently that the campaign was started with the slogan "START SEEING MOTORCYCLES!"

When the Minnesota license plate renewal forms are mailed out, the Department of Transportation includes an insert along with the registration form. The insert has a dot on the left side of the page, with instructions telling you to cover your left eye and look at the right side of the page. When you do, the dot disappears, even though it is still there. The point of the exercise is to teach drivers to be constantly on the lookout for motorcycles that are there but are often not seen. It works. I've noticed that there seem to be many more motorcycles on the road these days.

God is there, whether we see Him or not. Two people can look at the same page of history; one sees God and the other doesn't. But God is always there and always making a difference.

Faith is opening our eyes to God. Those who value faith practice looking around more than those who don't value faith. Suddenly there is the startling discovery that the image and actions of God are visible in people, events, places, and things that previously seemed godless. Faith is seeing God.

START SEEING GOD!

Questions

For Thought:

1. What part does faith play in your life when your prayers—for healing, for saving a marriage, for a loved one's salvation—are not answered the way you want them to be?

2. Think about this statement: "Those who value faith look for every opportunity to trust God." When difficulties arise in your life, do you see them as an opportunity to trust God, or do you complain and worry instead? Why?

3. Name at least one thing in your life that you are tempted to complain or worry about, and ask God to give you the faith

to trust Him for the outcome. Are you excited that you have decided to exercise faith and trust God in your situation? Or are you uneasy about trusting God in this instance? Why?

For Discussion:

1. What are some situations in which a faulty understanding of faith can have damaging consequences?
2. Discuss some ways that we can open our eyes to God. Make a point this next week of looking for the image and action of God in people, places, events, and things. Be prepared next time to share with the group a few ways that you have discovered God where you might have missed Him before.
3. If I have faith, can I get what I want? What should be our response when we don't get what we want?
4. Why do some people have more faith than others?

Chapter 8

Doing Good

A PASTOR phoned the home of some recent church visitors. A voice answered with a whispered, "Hello."

Pastor: "Who is this?"

Whisper: "Jimmy."

Pastor: "How old are you, Jimmy?"

Whisper: "Four."

"Jimmy, may I please speak to your mom?"

"She's busy."

"Then may I speak to your dad?"

"He's busy."

"Are there any other adults at your home?"

"The police."

"Then let me speak to one of the police officers."

"They're busy."

"Who else is there?"

"Firemen."

"Well, put one of the firemen on the phone."

"They're busy."

"Jimmy, what are they all busy doing?"

"They're looking for me."

Just like Jimmy, a lot of people are hiding. Not only from parents and police, but from God. And there is nothing funny about hiding from the One who loves us most and the One we need the most.

Often we hide from God because we don't feel we measure up. We know we've done wrong. And no matter how hard we try, we think God is never satisfied.

There's nothing new to such hiding. It began in the Garden of Eden when Adam and Eve first sinned. God came looking for them and called out, "Where are you?" Adam whispered, "I heard you in the garden, and I was afraid . . . so I hid."

This initial act of sin raised the most profound question of human history: How do we get right with God? Millions of people have tried to win His favor by doing good, only to discover that our good never measures up to God's standards of perfection.

Martin Luther said that even after he had earned a Doctor of Theology degree he still didn't know how to get rid of his sin and get right with God. He tried every good work he could do and nothing was ever good enough. Then he turned to the straightforward truths of the Bible and discovered how to get in touch with God and how to do good.

Connecting Up With God—Grace

Because God is perfect, His standard is perfection. Because we are all sinners, everything we do is imperfect. This difference creates an enormous human dilemma.

Have you ever played the amusement park game where you swing a huge hammer and try to make the ball shoot up to ring the bell? When it comes to that one, I prefer to watch. Who wants to pay good money to try as hard as you can in order to be publicly rated a "wimp"? But I've watched young muscular guys swing with all their might and weight (and anger) without coming close.

That's what people do who try to work their way to God. They attend church, give money, and do charity—without ever getting close to ringing the bell of God.

The Bible clearly tells us that nobody has what it takes to ever measure up to God's perfection. So what are we supposed to do? Hide?

The answer is found in one of the most important statements in God's Word: "For it is by grace you have been saved, through faith—and this is not from yourselves, it is the gift of God—not by works, so that no one can boast" (Ephesians 2:8–9).

This is the central core of Christianity: God's generous gift to solve the human dilemma was the substitution of His perfect Son. In other words, God allowed Jesus to stand in for us. In our weakness we could not ring the bell, but Jesus could and did. He measured up. And He died—paying the penalty for our sin.

Getting God doesn't depend on our good works. It depends on His generosity. It's a gift. Expensive for God but free for us. And we accept it by faith, by believing.

This is really how a person becomes a Christian. It's how I became a Christian. One day I realized that nothing I could ever do was good enough, so I told God that I believed and accepted. I believed in Jesus as my Savior and accepted God's gift of eternal life.

Have you done the same? Do you remember when? Are you sure you've become a Christian? Have you told God you believe and accept? Don't answer by telling of something good you did—like going to church or being baptized or helping someone. Be sure that you have told God you believe and accept. Be sure you are a Christian.

Doing Good Works

As soon as a person believes and becomes a Christian, good works take on a completely different meaning. Instead of being not good enough, instead of being a false hope for some people, good works become a very important part of life to the Christian.

Ephesians 2:10 explains that "we are God's workmanship, created in Christ Jesus to do good works, which God prepared in advance for us to do." In other words, once we become Christians ("created in Christ Jesus"), the design of our lives is to do things that are good.

In fact, good works in the Christian's life is a major theme of the New Testament:

Christians are to be "eager to do what is good" (Titus 2:14).

Christians are to "devote themselves to doing what is good" (Titus 3:8).

The purpose of the Bible is to teach and rebuke and correct and train us so that we may be "thoroughly equipped for every good work" (2 Timothy 3:17).

Jesus said that Christians are to be "the light of the world," although many don't remember how Jesus said we should do that. He said, "Let your light shine before men, that they may see your good deeds and praise your Father in heaven" (Matthew 5:16).

James gets into the debate over people who say "I have faith" but don't show any evidence of it. He explains that "faith by itself, if it is not accompanied by action, is dead" (James 2:17).

Then, in the very last chapter of the Bible, Jesus ties everything together, saying, "Behold, I am coming soon! My reward is with me, and I will give to everyone according to what he has done" (Revelation 22:12). Rewards for good workers!

According to God's Word, doing good works is an essential part of the Christian life and, therefore, essential to anyone who is a Christian.

Four key concepts summarize the value of good works in the life of a Christian:

1. Good works are valuable because they are required for being like Jesus. Christians are to behave Christianly, and Christ did good.

2. A Christian does good for God. That's why it's possible to do good for people who are ungrateful, undeserving, or resistant. The skeptic who doesn't understand Christian thinking may ask, "How can you be so kind to that creep?" But we know we are exercising kindness primarily for God's sake and only secondarily for the sake of the undeserving recipient of the kindness. As a Christian I can do good for someone who is rotten to me because I don't treat other people on the basis of the

way they treat me. I treat others on the basis of the way Jesus treats me. Big difference!

3. Good works are evidence a person is a Christian. Though all good works are not done only by Christians, anyone who claims to be a Christian and doesn't act like a Christian probably isn't a Christian. Those who claim to be Christians and behave like Christians probably are Christians.

4. Good works have an inside and an outside. The inside of good works is motive and the outside of good works is action. With other people I can only see the outside and guess at the inside. With myself I can know the inside.

Is it possible to have the motive of love on the inside and botch the action on the outside? Of course it is. I've done that—really been motivated by the love of Jesus Christ and done something that came off poorly and was greatly misunderstood. It especially hurts when we are rightly motivated but accused by others of wrong motivation because of their misunderstanding.

It is also possible to be selfishly and sinfully motivated on the inside but look very good on the outside. I've done that, too. I've been credited for being a super-nice guy when my actions were wrongly motivated.

The best way is to get good works right on the inside and the outside. Second best is to get them right on the inside even if they don't always come out right on the outside. What you really don't want is to be selfishly and sinfully motivated on the inside, no matter how it appears on the outside.

Let's get specific. What would you put on a list of good works that flow out of being a Christian? Here are a few possibilities:

Forgiveness: Think of someone who has really hurt you. Choose to forgive that person and treat him or her with warmth whether that person likes it or not. That would be just like Jesus, wouldn't it?

Kindness: Do something kind for someone without expecting anything in return—not even thanks. Mow a lawn. Help paint. Baby-sit. Help someone find a job. Give a gift. Send a card. Make a phone call.

I know someone who considered an opportunity to do a

Christian kindness and decided to entertain a family with eight children for dinner because they probably were never invited out.

Time: Time is more valuable to some people than money. To whom and where could time be given as a good deed? Helping in the church nursery perhaps. Sitting with a bedridden patient in a nursing home. Tutoring underprivileged children.

Generosity: How much money do you give away? Did you know that in terms of percentages, the poorest Americans give the most and the richest give the least? Who is poor, lonely, messed up, sick, grieving, depressed, undeserving, ungrateful, hungry, unemployed, frightened, alienated, desperate, sinful? What good could be done to help?

Justice: Where is there injustice that could be corrected by good works? Too many people can't get jobs because of the unwillingness of companies to take risks in inner cities. Mortgages are unavailable to minorities because of informal but illegal "redlining" by lenders. Prejudice prevails in most quarters of our society as racism rises. The Christian who has power to influence corporate and civic decisions toward justice should do so for God and for those created in His image. It is always a good work to confront injustice and to advance justice.

The list is endless. Opportunities for good works are as numerous as people in the world and hours in our lives. Because we are Christians we value good works. We believe that giving is more valuable than getting. We believe that good works are more valuable than money, that serving others is more valuable than being famous or important, that position and power are to be used to help others rather than to promote ourselves.

This is a very different value system than that of non-Christians. It's not that we feel great pressure. It's not because we've been shamed into doing good. We're Christians. We want to be like Jesus. Therefore, we not only value doing good but we love doing good for Jesus.

Imagine what could happen if an explosion of good works were to happen among individual Christians as well as in the church and out into the world. Compare this to the popularity of Bible studies. There must be a million or more home Bible studies each week in the United States. Christians gather with friends to read and discuss some section of the Old or New Testaments. What if there were an equal number of Christian "Good Works Groups"—weekly meetings of Christian neighbors and friends to plan and then implement acts of good works in their communities and beyond? Nothing could be more practical. God would be delighted and a lot of good would be done.

I recently met an African-American man from Ohio whose job transfer had taken him first to Chicago and then to a large southern city. Although he was a layman working in the business world, he started a church. Within four years, the church had grown to a congregation of one thousand, comprised of middle to upper-middle class African-Americans. Needing more room, the church bought a building from a church that was disbanding. The building was located in a poor all-white neighborhood that was the center of Ku Klux Klan activity in that southern state. The church's move precipitated animosity, threats, violence, and other expressions of racism.

The pastor and people of the African-American church prayed and decided that they needed to undertake good deeds that would enable them to win members of the Ku Klux Klan to Jesus Christ. They determined that the professionals in the church could help the poor whites get bank loans, set up small businesses, network government aid, overcome unemployment and underemployment. They offered their help through seminars, counseling, networking, and friendships. The white KKKers wouldn't come into the church building, so the church rented space in a neutral part of the city. And an unusual and effective ministry began and continues today.

I think this pastor and his church are just like Jesus, because it sounds to me like the kind of thing Jesus would do.

I think they understand what being Christian really means—they have faith and they're acting it out.

I think they value and practice Christian good works.

I think that's the kind of Christian I want to be.

Questions

For Thought:

1. Are you sure you have become a Christian? Have you accepted God's free gift of forgiveness from sin and eternal life according to Ephesians 2:8–9? Or do you hide from God because you don't feel you measure up?
2. If you are certain that you are a Christian and have accepted God's free gift by grace, then ask yourself if you are still trusting God to save you by grace, or have you begun to trust in your "good works" to make you right with God?
3. Having been made right with God through grace, the life of a Christian should be filled with good works—as an outward reflection of what has happened on the inside. Is this happening in your life now? In what ways?

For Discussion:

1. Discuss the value of good works in the life of a Christian.
2. Read out loud the list of ideas for "good works" on pages 105–106. Does this list help you think of some new ideas for doing good that you haven't thought of before? Talk about those ideas together.
3. Discuss the possibility of creating a group committed to doing good works for non-Christians.

Chapter 9

More Than a Feeling

WHEN FREDDY and Helen Johnson turned fifty, they decided to give up their executive home in metropolitan Raleigh, North Carolina, along with their three BMWs and much of their expensive clothing. "I climbed the ladder of success all my life, only to discover that my ladder was leaning against the wrong building," commented Freddy Johnson.

The Johnsons moved into downtown Raleigh across from the Halifax housing project and started Building Together Ministries. They live in a busy two-bedroom house that attracts lots of neighbors and friends. Their ministry has a thrift store, a computer center, and provides after-school activities for neighborhood children and youth.

When the Johnsons accompanied ten African-American neighborhood youths to a North Carolina camp, the camp leader asked the teens, "Tell me something about Freddy." One of the girls spoke for the others and said, "Freddy? Oh, he just loves us."

Later the camp leader said, "With racial tension on the increase, what a model for reconciliation for these black youths to see a white man as someone who loves Jesus and simply loves them."

The price of love? Freddy Johnson answers, "Who would have imagined that steps of downward mobility could give the inner peace, joy, and contentment I had searched for all my life?"[1]

"Love" has to be one of the most used and most difficult to define words in our English language. My dictionary lists eleven different definitions. It is a noun and a verb. It refers to sex, romance, God, and tennis. In romance, love is everything. In tennis, love is nothing.

Picture a young couple who have been dating. The relationship has grown serious. They have gone out for dinner and are now seated together on a lakeside park bench on a warm moonlit night. Finally he gets enough courage to say that he loves her, but he wants to make sure she knows exactly what he means, so he holds her hand, looks into her eyes, and says, "I have tender and passionate affection for you as one of the opposite sex." Somehow the dictionary doesn't quite capture all that love is about, does it?

Old Testament Hebrew has only one word for love, *aheb*. New Testament Greek, however, has several:

Storge means natural affection, especially between a mother and a child. We know there is a difference between love of a child and love of a mate, but in our language we have to use the same word.

Philia is the love word for affection between friends and those we really like. It's too bad we don't have a love word like "philia" in English, because many of us feel uncomfortable saying "I love you" to a good friend or a brother or sister. We feel the affection but we don't have a good word to describe it.

Eros is the love word for strong attraction, especially sexual love. In our vocabulary we often refer to sexual intercourse as "making love." We know this is not the same as the other kinds of love, but it is one of the definitions of this all-purpose word.

Agape is another Greek word for love, although it was rarely

[1]"Down the Ladder to Success," *Urban Family*, Vol. 2, No. 1 (Spring 1993), 17–18.

used in New Testament times. Agape is an extreme love that gives unselfishly for the benefit of another person. While feelings are part of agape, action is especially important.

All four kinds of love are gifts from God. Some people abuse one kind or another, but in original design and intent every one is wonderful.

The first three kinds of love are by far the easiest to experience and express because they are based on the attraction to the ones we love and the benefits we ourselves can get in return for that love.

We love our children and our parents because we are related to them and enjoy being loved back. We love our friends because we see something in them that we like and because we get lots of good returns from those friendships. We love sexually because we are physically attracted to another person and receive sexual pleasure and satisfaction out of the relationship.

Agape love is different. It is centered on the person who is doing the loving, not the person being loved. It is all for giving and not for getting. It is completely to benefit another rather than to get benefit for oneself. Agape love is great to get but supernatural to give.

But first let's think in terms of receiving more than giving love.

The Best We Can Get

Everyone loves to be loved. We all want other people to be drawn to us, to want to be with us, to want to do good for us. Wanting to be loved is expressed in many different ways. Some of us just want to be held. We want to be important in someone else's life. We want to be needed. We like having someone stand up for us.

The problem is that most love is based on our personal desirability. If we look good, we are sexually attractive. If we behave in the ways our parents approve, we think we will retain their love. If we keep a husband or wife happy, they will love us for doing so. If we have money or something else people want, they will love us.

Wouldn't it be great just to be loved for yourself? Wouldn't it be wonderful if someone could know the "real you" and love you anyway? What if someone could see into your soul, know everything about you on the inside, and still love you? What if you could be loved even when you say and do stupid, awful things? What if someone would just love you for you, the way you are?

There is only one kind of love that loves us "as is," and that is agape love. And God is the only source for agape love. Romans 5:7–8 explains: "Very rarely will anyone die for a righteous man, though for a good man someone might possibly dare to die. But God demonstrates his own love for us in this: While we were still sinners, Christ died for us."

This gets right to the point. For whom would you die? Many people wouldn't die for anyone under any circumstances. Some heroes would be willing to die for someone really, really special and very good. We *might* be willing to die for a child we are really devoted to or a friend who is absolutely wonderful or a dearly loved husband or wife. But most of us would not love and be willing to die for a child who hates us and has made life miserable, or a friend who has betrayed and bankrupted us, or a spouse who has abused us, committed adultery, or divorced us.

Yet that is exactly the way God has loved every one of us. He loved us in spite of our rebellion and sin against Him. He loved us knowing every bad thing about every one of us. He demonstrated His love for us by having Jesus Christ die for us even though we were sinners.

When you read a used car ad in the newspaper and it says "as is," you know there is something seriously wrong with that vehicle. Recently our family was shopping for a minivan and found a nearly new Dodge Caravan with only 3,000 miles on it for a very low price. It had been repurchased by the Chrysler Corporation under the "Lemon Law." The dealer told us the first owners had transmission troubles and returned the car but that since then a whole new transmission had been installed. He assured us it was literally better than new. But we never drove the car or even looked inside it. I've had enough cars that ended up being lemons without starting out with one officially designated a lemon. We didn't want it at any price.

The amazing thing about God's love is not just that He loved us and bought us "as is," knowing we were lemons; the truly amazing thing is that He was willing to pay top price for us. He paid the most exorbitant price ever charged: the suffering and death of His own Son. That is agape love that is so amazing it is outrageous.

The main point about the agape love of God is not how God feels, but what God does. The real test of all love is action, not words or feelings. If someone says "I love you" and behaves in an unloving fashion, don't believe it is real love.

Of course, love always involves feelings. God has feelings of great affection for us. I'm glad He does. But because of sin, God can also get angry with us. Because of His agape love, though, He treats us right even if we treat Him wrong.

God acted out His love to humans:

> This is how God showed his love among us: He sent his one and only Son into the world that we might live through him. This is love: not that we loved God, but that he loved us and sent his Son as an atoning sacrifice for our sins. (1 John 4:9–10)

This is not natural behavior! It is not natural to love someone who doesn't love you. It is not natural to give your best to someone who doesn't even care. It is not natural to give when there is no guarantee you will receive anything in return. This is supernatural behavior. This is supernatural love. It's the best we can get. It stretches our imagination to understand the way God loves us.

How do we handle this? How do we respond? What do we do when God loves us so much?

The Best We Can Give

One day a very smart lawyer asked Jesus, "What is the greatest thing a person can do?" Jesus answered, " 'Love the Lord your God with all your heart and with all your soul and with all your mind.' This is the first and greatest commandment. And the second is like it: 'Love your neighbor as yourself' " (Matthew 22:37–39).

The best thing we can do in life is love God. The second best thing we can do in life is love others the way God loves us. Loving others means loving them "as is." It means loving the lemons. It means loving them even if they hate us. It means loving them on the basis of the love coming out of us rather than on the basis of anything attractive about them. It means loving them whether they want to be loved or not.

This is the greatest opportunity we could ever have.

It is our opportunity to thank God by loving like God.

It is our opportunity to be like God by loving like God.

It is our opportunity to complete the love of God by passing it on to others.

One of the most profound mysteries of Christianity is the invisibility of God and how we can know He is real even if we cannot see Him. First John 4:12 explains that "no one has ever seen God; but if we love each other, God lives in us and his love is made complete in us."

People can't see God. But they can see the love of God in us when we behave just like God. This does not come naturally (as when we love the lovable), but supernaturally (when we love the unlovable). It somehow completes the love of God in us. It shows us the God that we could not otherwise see and proves that the love of God in us is real. Loving others confirms our Christian faith in a tangible way.

Do you have any Christmas tree lights that are wired in series? The ones that don't work if a bulb is loose or burned out? The electricity flows to the first bulb and then through the first bulb to the second and so on until they all light up. If every bulb both receives and sends electricity, the entire string shines brightly.

God designed Christians to be wired together in a similar fashion. The love of God supernaturally flows into us. When the flow of love goes out of us to others, "his love is made complete in us." It shines brightly, giving us the wonderful opportunity not only to be loved but to love like God. Not only to get love but to give love.

Jesus said that the greatest single evidence that a person is a Christian is getting love and giving love: "Love one another. As I have loved you, so you must love one another. All men will know that you are my disciples if you love one another" (John 13:34–35).

Notice that Jesus never said His disciples would be known by their church membership or denomination or by making financial donations. *The* evidence of a Christian being a follower of Christ is getting and giving His love.

The Crow Wing Power and Light Company in central Minnesota has this advice to employees printed inside the company operating manual: "People don't care how much you know; they want to know how much you care." Of course, customers want the CWP&L employees to know enough about electricity to provide uninterrupted power to their homes. But there's a lot of truth in the "care" part as well. Many Americans are weary of a technological age that overvalues knowledge and undervalues love. We all want to be loved.

Unfortunately, to be blunt, this is not always the way Christians order their values. We are prone to give higher priority to other cultural and Christian values as evidence of faith. Persons are judged to be true believers based upon their religious knowledge and their compliance with biblical practices such as church attendance, prayer, Bible reading, or spiritual gifts. Or they are judged to be true believers based upon their moral convictions and political activity related to abortion, homosexuality, capital punishment, divorce, drug abuse, or some other volatile current issue.

Please understand clearly: These are all very important. They may, in fact, be the specific arenas where love is lived out. However, to be truly Christian in those settings, showing love must be *more important* than winning arguments or votes or legislation.

What does it mean when a professed Christian writes an unloving letter to a magazine castigating a person for immoral behavior or unjust political positions? Tragically, the failure to live Christianly and write lovingly not only undermines the impact of the letter, but contradicts the claim to be a follower of Jesus Christ.

At the other extreme are those devout Christians who speak and exercise love toward those with whom they disagree, including individuals who totally disregard Christian values. It is impossible to overestimate the power and persuasion of love in the ugliest of confrontations. But far more important is the sheer virtue of loving like God, independent of the hatred expressed by others.

I recall the way one husband acted when his wife became a Christian. He did everything he could to provoke her, treating her unkindly and unjustly for years. Her consistent responses of love in the face of hate irritated him to higher levels of provocation. I heard him say that he became obsessed with making her life miserable and forcing her Christianity to crumble. His behavior particularly focused on stopping her from going to church, reading the Bible, giving away money, or praying. He actually gathered up all her Bibles and Christian literature and burned them in the backyard while his wife and children were forced to watch. He forbid family members from going to church, hiding the car keys or blocking the doorway. He threatened dire consequences if anyone in his home was caught praying.

Eventually, however, this man realized he was up against a power far greater than his evil. He was stunned and overwhelmed by his wife's love for him, expressed in a thousand different ways. He finally gave in, saying, "If that's what Christianity is like, I want to become a Christian."

There is a temptation at this point to list specific ways for us to live the love of God. The trouble is that such lists tilt toward legalism. They can become checklists that are outwardly performed without inward love. If a person does not first love God, no list of suggestions will make any significant difference. The best that legalistic lists usually do is produce guilt and condemnation. We feel guilty for not measuring up, and we condemn others for not doing what we ourselves are unable to do.

Let's consider a different approach. Assume that any lack of love in a Christian's life comes primarily from a lack of feeling loved by God. Instead of trying to love others in order to get loved by God, do the opposite. Go to Him to get "loved up." Receive the love of God. Get so full of God's love that it spills out all over everybody else.

How does a person get filled with God's love? Here's a place where a list might be appropriate.

- Read about the love of God in the Bible until you are overwhelmed by the truth of how much He loves you.
- Spend blocks of time meditating with God about how much He loves you just the way you are.
- Quit trying to measure up. Quit trying to impress God. Admit you don't have anything to offer. Accept how much He loves you just for you.
- Pray and thank God for His love. Thank Him at least a few thousand times. Spend time just thinking and feeling and accepting the love of God in your life.
- Allow God just to love you, love you, love you. Become so aware of how little you deserve the love of God and so full of that love that you begin to see others as God sees you and love others as God loves you.
- Start getting loved up by God right this minute. And make this a priority this week—and for the rest of life.
- Value the love of God in your life. It's the best you can get . . . and it's the best you can give.

In the middle of the Bible's major teaching on spiritual gifts we find the 1 Corinthians 13 love chapter. Suddenly there is a subtle but important switch in terminology. After using "gifts" to refer to faith, evangelism, leadership, teaching, tongues, and healings, Paul says, "And now I will show you the most excellent way" (1 Corinthians 12:31). What follows, then, is his teaching that all Christian activities—from the mundane to the spectacular—are relatively unimportant compared to the highly valued way of love that should permeate every Christian's thoughts and actions:

> If I speak in the tongues of men and of angels, but have not love, I am only a resounding gong or a clanging cymbal. If I have the gift of prophecy and can fathom all mysteries and all knowledge, and if I have a faith that can move mountains, but have not love, I am nothing. If I give all I possess to the poor and surrender my body to the flames, but have not love, I gain nothing.
>
> Love is patient, love is kind. It does not envy, it does not boast, it is not proud. It is not rude, it is not self-seeking, it is not easily angered, it keeps no record of wrongs. Love does not delight in evil but rejoices with the truth. It always

protects, always trusts, always hopes, always perseveres.

Love never fails. But where there are prophecies, they will cease; where there are tongues, they will be stilled; where there is knowledge, it will pass away. For we know in part and we prophesy in part, but when perfection comes, the imperfect disappears. When I was a child, I talked like a child, I thought like a child, I reasoned like a child. When I became a man, I put childish ways behind me. Now we see but a poor reflection; then we shall see face to face. Now I know in part; then I shall know fully, even as I am fully known.

And now these three remain: faith, hope and love. But the greatest of these is love. (1 Corinthians 13:1–13)

God is love. God highly values love. God loves.

We are loved by God. We love God. We highly value love. We love others.

Questions

For Thought:

1. Read again the list of suggestions on page 117 for how to get "loved up" by God. Think of some other ways of getting filled with God's love that you have never tried.
2. Think of a person you are having a hard time loving. Ask God to love that person through you—even in some small way.
3. What are some tangible ways you can express *agape* love to others in your family, church, or workplace?

For Discussion:

1. Discuss the differences between the four Greek words for "love": *storge, philia, eros,* and *agape.*
2. Romans 5:7–8 states: "Very rarely will anyone die for a righ-

teous man, though for a good man someone might possibly dare to die. But God demonstrates his own love for us in this: While we were still sinners, Christ died for us." God has loved us "as is." What does that mean to you?

3. Discuss some ways a person can get filled with God's love so that it spills out all over everybody else.

Chapter 10

Sharing the Values

LIFE CAN BE a roller-coaster ride of ecstatic highs and empty lows. Remember the happiest day in your life, when you were surprised by joy? Remember the saddest day in your life, when you were racked with disappointment? If you are like most of us, you wanted someone to tell. Someone to share your joy and happiness. Someone to share your pain and loss.

Whether sharing the highs or the lows, that sharing is what we call fellowship. The Greeks called it *koinonia*, a multifaceted word that has several different English translations: "sharing, participating, communion, friendship." Whichever definition is used, however, it is always based on the concept of fellowship that grows out of having something in common. There must be a common denominator for fellowship/koinonia to occur.

Just watch any group of strangers as they become acquainted with one another. Everyone looks for some common bond for friendship. Often people will group together by age, or gender, or race, or nationality, or mutual friendships, or similar experience, or common interest.

We all delight in finding someone who grew up near us,

someone who attended the same school, someone who cheers for the same professional sports team. If we can't find some common bond, we usually break off the relationship. Where there is nothing in common there can be no real fellowship.

Think of it in mathematical terms. Compare three fractions: $\frac{1}{2}$, $\frac{1}{3}$, $\frac{214}{400}$. Which two have the most in common? At first glance the $\frac{1}{2}$ and the $\frac{1}{3}$ look the most alike and the $\frac{214}{400}$ is the weird one. But after a closer look you see that the $\frac{1}{2}$ and $\frac{1}{3}$ only look alike while the $\frac{1}{2}$ and $\frac{214}{400}$ share a common denominator of 2. That common denominator makes them much easier to add together.

Fellowship works the same way. It is based on a common denominator. Sometimes it is obvious and easy to find. Sometimes it is difficult to find. But if there is nothing in common, there can be no fellowship.

Actually, the whole idea of fellowship begins with God.

Fellowship of the Trinity

The Bible teaches that in the beginning there was God. Just God. God never began. God always was. This sounds both boring and lonely, but God was neither.

From forever ago God existed as three persons. We call them Father, Son, and Spirit. They had one all-important thing in common: they were all God. Because they had their deity in common, they fellowshiped together. They shared everything. They participated in projects together, including the creation of the universe and our world.

Because fellowship is so central and essential to who God is, and because we are created in His image, we have been designed for fellowship. We all have a natural and normal need for fellowship with other human beings.

After God created Adam and Eve, He just naturally fellowshiped with them. They talked together. They worked on projects together. They had a great time together because of all they had in common.

Tragically, Adam and Eve broke fellowship with God. They chose to sin. God is holy and sinless. He hates sin. So God could no longer fellowship with Adam and Eve as before. When He came to the Garden to share with His human friends, everyone immediately knew something was wrong. Their fellowship was broken.

There is no way for us to understand the profound loss God experienced in this loss of fellowship. He had created Adam and Eve to be like Him so they could be friends, but the primary basis of their common denominator had been broken. Because of sin they were too different for the old fellowship to continue.

The closest comparable human emotion may be that which is felt by a parent estranged from a son or daughter. A man and woman want a child who will be like them, who will share their home, values, and dreams. A son or daughter is born, and during the early years of childhood it seems as if the dream has come true. But then, during adolescence, the child of their dreams chooses drugs, friends, and activities that alienate him from his parents. The relationship becomes strained. Now there are more differences than similarities, more expressions of hatred than of love. Those who once were close become like strangers with little in common. The parents' hearts ache over broken dreams and a lost relationship.

God wanted fellowship with humanity restored because He valued that relationship and He valued His creation. But putting fellowship back together again was not a simple or easy thing to do. It required the sacrifice of God's only Son, Jesus Christ. Jesus became the new common denominator in order to restore the lost fellowship with us humans. "God, who has called you into fellowship with his Son Jesus Christ our Lord, is faithful" (1 Corinthians 1:9). And through the death and resurrection of Jesus, those who believe on Him become the new children of God—like new Adams and Eves. "And our fellowship is with the Father and with his Son, Jesus Christ" (1 John 1:3).

This may not sound like a big deal, but it is. It is, in fact, the biggest deal. We can share with God. We can talk with God. We can participate in God's work and God can participate in our work. Fellowship with God means friendship with God. It's the best we can get. It's worth everything. It's more than valuable. It is invaluable.

Christian Fellowship=Sharing/Participating

Christian fellowship with God is based on what we have in common with God, Jesus Christ. A Christian is someone who has a personal relationship with God through Jesus. And just as every Christian has Jesus as the common denominator with God, so every Christian has Jesus as the common denominator with other believers.

It's like being members of the same family. We are all spiritually related and connected through Jesus Christ. We're all brothers and sisters. What we have in common is not language, gender, education, employment, ZIP code, or citizenship. It is Jesus. "There is neither Jew nor Greek, slave nor free, male nor female, for you are all one in Christ Jesus" (Galatians 3:28).

As Christians we highly value the relationship we have with each other based on Jesus. "We have come to share in Christ . . ." (Hebrews 3:14). It's enough to make us love people we might not otherwise like. It's enough to draw us close to people who would otherwise be complete strangers. It's enough to motivate us to forgive when otherwise we might stay angry.

It is important to understand that Christian fellowship is never primarily based on having children the same age, on living in the same neighborhood, on working for the same company, or on going to the same church. What draws us together and glues us together is Jesus. He is our reason for friendship. He is the subject of our conversations. He is the One for whom we all love to work.

Just as good fellowship is wonderful, bad fellowship is awful. God's Word warns Christians, "Do not be yoked together with unbelievers. For what do righteousness and wickedness have in common? Or what fellowship can light have with darkness? . . . What does a believer have in common with an unbeliever?" (2 Corinthians 6:14–15).

This does not forbid friendships with non-Christians, but it does say that there cannot be a soul-bond to an unbeliever. There is an inherent danger for a Christian marrying, becoming a business partner with, or even a best friend with a non-Christian. Although some Christians have taken this beyond the biblical intent, the primary teaching here is that Christians should beware of entering into fellowship relationships with non-Christians. It is especially dangerous if either unbeliever or the relationship has greater influence on the Christian than the Christian has on the unbeliever and the relationship.

Sometimes, of course, Christians have no choice. In the first century, Christian slaves were sold to non-Christian slaveholders and forced into a binding relationship with an unbeliever. Even in our modern society, some cultures still insist on weddings arranged by parents, thereby at times forcing Christians into marriages with unbelievers. In such extreme cases the believer has an even greater challenge, and this becomes an opportunity to experience God's special help and use the situation for God's greater good. The higher principle that applies in every relationship is to be sure to "not share in the sins of others" (1 Timothy 5:22).

This is certainly not to say that all natural associations are wrong or unimportant. Of course there are bases for fellowship other than Christian faith. At international Christian conferences the delegates from Japan usually stay in the same hotel, eat meals together, and sit together during meetings. At church gatherings the parents of school-age children often prefer each other's fellowship because they are in the same chapter of life and dealing with many of the same issues. However, Christian values require us to order our assignment of importance to relationships. The most important basis for fellowship is a common denominator of Jesus Christ, which means that we have more in common with another Christian even of a different race, age, and gender than we have with a non-Christian of our same race, age, and gender. If that is not true, if we give higher priority to natural associations than to supernatural associations, we are ordering the values of life in ways that do not reflect God's values.

To round out our understanding of fellowship requires us to move from thinking of fellowship as primarily a passive relationship. Just as marriage is not primarily a legal document and family is not a set of birth certificates, fellowship is not merely being Christians listed on the Rolodex of heaven. Marriage and family and fellowship are all active relationships: they describe what we do with specific relationships we have.

Fellowship may be a noun in the dictionary, but it is a verb to those who live Christianly.

Fellowship . . . Do It!

When we truly value something, we take initiative regarding it. If we value money, we save it or invest it. If we value books, we buy them and read them. If we value food, we eat it. And if we value fellowship, we do it.

This means we regularly reach out to establish relationships that share life with other Christians. A Christian without fellowship is an oxymoron; it just doesn't make sense.

Too many Christians miss out on the God-given value of fellowship because they spend a lifetime waiting for someone to fellowship with them. Other Christians miss out on God's fellowship because they build all their relationships on jobs or hobbies or common denominators other than Christ.

Don't wait any longer. Don't lay the responsibility on the church or other Christians. Take the initiative to share life with other Christians through fellowship together, and the place to begin is with a focus on Christ and on giving of our time, of ourselves. If we enter into relationships with other Christians with our primary focus on fellowship itself rather than on Christ, or on what we can get rather than on what we can give, we're bound to be disappointed.

I've lived around Christians and churches all my life. And I've seen hundreds of Christians come to a church looking for great fellowship and expecting to get a lot from other people. They are almost always disappointed. Many of them spend a lifetime looking, often becoming bitter and angry people. Why? Because people and churches never measure up to those kinds of expectations.

I've also seen hundreds of Christians who are focused on Jesus and what they can give of themselves to others. Those people are not disappointed. They are far less likely to end up bitter and angry. They come out winners.

Calls to this high value of Christian fellowship are woven throughout the New Testament:

Selling their possessions and goods, they gave to anyone as he had need. (Acts 2:45)

The New Testament often speaks about those who gave away what they had to those in need but rarely mentions those in need getting anything. The emphasis was on giving.

All the believers were one in heart and mind. No one claimed that any of his possessions was his own, but they shared everything they had. (Acts 4:32)

Share with God's people who are in need. (Romans 12:13)

Carry each other's burdens. (Galatians 6:2)

And do not forget to do good and to share with others, for with such sacrifices God is pleased. (Hebrews 13:16)

Consider some of these practical suggestions for translating these first-century biblical principles and practices into modern acts of Christian fellowship:

- Befriend someone who needs a friend—not for what you'll get, but in order to give.
- Offer to pray with and for someone who has a special need.
- Whenever you hear about a job opening at your company, pass the word along to others looking for work.
- Give away your car instead of trading it in. Don't give it to a charitable organization to get a tax deduction. Give it to some Christian who needs a car and can't afford to buy one.
- Offer your week of time-share vacation or the use of your cabin to someone who really needs a vacation.
- Pay someone's medical bills. If you know they don't have adequate money or insurance, just mail a check to the doctor or hospital and ask for it to be credited to the account of the person who needs help.
- When you know a Christian in financial need, help out. Give some cash or a check. Consider sending it anonymously if that's appropriate. Since the United States Internal Revenue Service does not allow gifts going to individuals to be tax deductible, don't try to circumvent the

law by giving through a church or other charitable organization.

- Use your professional skills to help someone who can't
afford to pay—like the dentist who offered free care to
the child of a recently divorced single mother. Or the re-
tired handyman who does home repairs for widows one
day each week.

- Volunteer to drive someone who regularly needs a ride to
the doctor or to church.

- Phone an elderly shut-in at 8:00 A.M. every day (or some
other set time) to make sure that he or she is okay and
feels loved and not forgotten.

All of this is helping to bear one another's burdens. Don't
expect the government to do it. Don't expect the church to do
it. Don't expect someone else to do it. Just try doing it yourself.
We have forsaken too much individual responsibility to institutions. Skip the institutions. Fellowship, share, and participate.
That's what they did in the New Testament church.

Also join with others in ministry. Ministering together is a
wonderful means of fellowship. It forces us not only to work
together, but to trust God together. Teach Sunday school. Build
a house with Habitat for Humanity. Set up a prayer group on
behalf of non-Christians in your neighborhood, for a missionary in Latin America, or for the suffering people of Rwanda.

Look for fellowship relationships through a small group,
home Bible study, adult Sunday school class, or other gathering
of Christians.

Don't wait to be asked. Take the initiative. Focus on Christ.
Expect to give. Value fellowship.

Does Fellowship Mean Church Membership?

For most North American Christians the most practical issues of Christian fellowship are related to local churches. It is
not always easy or ideal to live out Christian relationships in a
local congregation. In fact, pollsters report increasing percentages of North Americans who claim to be growing Christians
yet who have no church affiliation, participation, or desire for
such. Reasons for lack of church relationship are many, but

most have to do with negative experiences in the past, strained interpersonal relationships, disagreement over church doctrine or practices, or a perception that the church and its ministry are irrelevant to the individual's life.

Certainly it is possible to be a Christian without church membership or participation, but it should not be considered normal. Christians who follow Jesus as Lord must share His values, and one thing He values greatly is the church.

Jesus founded the church as His body on earth. Just as the work of God and word of God were primarily represented on earth through Jesus' original body (His physical body) during His thirty-three-year life in Palestine, so the work and word of God are primarily represented on earth now through His second body (the church, His spiritual body). He intended that believers organize together into fellowship communities with Him at the head. These local churches were normal in the New Testament and have continued to be the primary expression of Christian community for the past 2,000 years.

When Christians who are searching for a church home ask me what they should look for, I tell them to look for a congregation where the Bible is taught and where they feel comfortable. Beyond that they should allow some latitude in terms of denomination and expression of doctrine. The chances of their finding a church that perfectly fits every one of their beliefs and desires are minimal. Besides, it is this very point that tests the value of fellowship. Those who truly value Christian fellowship will tolerate differences among believers in order to do fellowship. This has been true from the very beginning. Differences and disagreements were part of the fellowship of the apostles during the days of the early church recorded in the book of Acts, and among the churches of Corinth, Galatia, Philippi, Thessalonica, and many others.

Local churches are like families. It's true that in certain instances a person may be forced to disassociate from his or her own family—from parents, brothers and sisters, or sons and daughters. But surely this is only in the most extreme and unusual circumstances. The same standard of extreme exception should apply to church affiliation.

This does not mean that Christians must stay a lifetime with any particular local church. Increasingly churches are like chapters of life that open and close, changing with each stage of growth and maturity. A family may move from one church to another because of a job transfer or because of the specific educational needs of teenage children. When a move is made, however, it is important to apply Christian values to the process of change. The way a person changes churches is often more important than the change itself. The practice of open communication along with Christian love, forgiveness, and understanding will allow ongoing fellowship with individuals, even if they are part of different churches.

Formal church membership is expected by some churches, while others don't have any membership at all. The words "church membership" never appear in the Bible. They are a human invention used to formally express the more important informal affiliation that takes place through Christian fellowship. Some Christians never become church members but share the fellowship; others go through the ritual and are added to the church membership roll but never connect relationally or experience genuine fellowship. Without a doubt, the fellowship is more important than the membership.

It seems to me that Christians should desire to fit in with the church of God's choice for them as best they can. When I move to another state, I cheer for that state's sports teams. When I am a guest in someone's home, I try to follow their house rules and traditions. When I visit in another country, I do my best to fit in with their culture and customs. Since the Christian value of fellowship is so important, I also choose to live by the norms established in any particular local church. If that means membership, I join. If that means no membership, I'll choose to live without it. Submitting my will to others, getting along with fellow believers who are different, fitting in on the basis of Jesus Christ rather than past tradition—these are all tangible expressions of my commitment to Jesus Christ and to other Christians for whom Christ died.

Think of it this way. Suppose you are planning to go on a dream vacation with a group of people from your hometown. This trip will include a flight to Australia, a cruise to Tahiti, and a stopover in Hawaii. During the weeks before you leave you do everything you can to get ready. You visit the tanning booth to build up your tan. You exercise to get into good shape. You practice language study so that you can say "Good Day" as one word for greetings in Australia. You attend tour group meetings to get acquainted with your fellow travelers and plan your itinerary. Your group includes people from all walks of life with varied interests, backgrounds, and experiences. What you have in common is your dream vacation. All of this is exciting, fun, and good preparation. Getting ready is half the joy of going there.

As Christians, we all have a real dream vacation coming. Better than Hawaii, more exotic than Tahiti, and farther than Australia. It's heaven. Forever.

During the weeks and years before we leave for heaven, we do everything we can to get ready. We get in shape spiritually. We study what our destination will be like. And we get to know the others who are going. They come from all walks of life and have varied interests, backgrounds, and experiences. What we have in common is that we all belong to Jesus Christ. Sharing this time together is called Christian fellowship. It is part of the joy of going to heaven.

Questions

For Thought:

1. Think about what fellowship with God means. What does it mean to you to have a never-ending friendship with Someone who will never let you down, never give up on you, but rather love you, encourage you, and support you in the difficult times of this life?

2. Jesus is the bond that draws us together in fellowship. Have you started to form a "soul-bond" with anyone whose values and beliefs are not in line with your Christian faith? Will that

person's friendship build you up in your faith, tear you down, or maybe even destroy it?

For Discussion:

1. What must be the relationship of priorities regarding our natural associations and our supernatural associations?
2. Discuss what it means to fellowship. Remember that *fellowship* is an active verb, requiring action on our part. How will it "work out" in our everyday life at home, at work, or in a difficult situation?
3. What are some differences between fellowship and church membership?

Chapter 11

Letting Sin Go

SIXTEEN-YEAR-OLD Billy, from a fine Christian home, is a member of the National Honor Society and a gifted musician. When friends of his family went to Hawaii for a week's vacation, they were thrilled to have Billy baby-sit their six-year-old twin boys. The MacDonalds never would have dreamed that Billy would repeatedly sexually molest their children while they were enjoying the beaches of Maui.

The Reverend Bradley Clark is a heretic. After twenty years of successful ministry as pastor of three conservative churches, he began to read the ancient writings of second- and third-century Gnostics. Casual interest became personal conviction, and his beliefs about Jesus Christ and the doctrine of the Trinity veered far from historic Christian orthodoxy.

Christopher Long is an embezzler. During the three years he worked for the United Banks, he successfully stole over $23,000 and used the money to cover gambling debts.

Each of these people claims to be a Christian and confesses regret and repentance for his actions. If you were the MacDonalds, would you forgive Billy for assaulting your boys? If you were a member of Pastor Clark's church, would you forgive him for teaching heresy? If you were president of United Banks, would you forgive Chris Long for stealing bank funds?

Let's suppose each answer to these hypothetical cases is a thoughtful and prayerful "yes." Try some harder questions. Having forgiven Billy, would you allow him to baby-sit for your boys during your next trip? Having forgiven Pastor Clark, would you vote for him to continue his preaching ministry in your church? Having forgiven Chris Long, would you return him to a position handling money at your bank?

Alexander Pope, the eighteenth-century English poet, wrote that "to err is human, to forgive divine." The words are familiar to most of us, even though few know the story behind them. Earlier in his life, Pope loved Lady Mary Wortley Montagu. At first she encouraged him but later scorned him. He did not forgive her, often seeking revenge against her in his writings.

We have all encountered those who erred against us, including some who hurt us so badly that forgiveness seems impossible. Perhaps it was a parent who left emotional scars on our soul. Or a teacher who humiliated us in front of friends. It may have been an assailant who brutalized us or a thief who invaded our home. Maybe it was a business partner who broke a deal, a child who took advantage of our love, a friend who betrayed our trust. At one time or another, all of us have been hurt by someone—intentionally or unintentionally. With each hurt we have the opportunity to forgive or not forgive.

If we decide to forgive, what if the offender does it again? Should we forgive again? If we decide to forgive a second time, should we extend forgiveness to a third round?

The first-century rabbis taught that three was the limit. Their teaching was based on the writings of Amos, the Old Testament prophet, who said that God would three times forgive the transgressions of people from Damascus, Gaza, Tyre, Edom, Ammon, and Moab (Amos 1–2). The rabbis reasoned that if three is God's limit, we shouldn't try to outforgive God; three should be our limit as well.

Based on the rabbis' teaching, Peter asked Jesus, "Lord, how many times shall I forgive my brother when he sins against me? Up to seven times?" Peter was very generous, doubling the going rate plus one. Jesus answered, "I tell you, not seven times, but seventy-seven times" (Matthew 18:21–22). Peter must have been shocked into silence with Jesus' response. In that silence Jesus told a parable that carried this compelling message: We should forgive others as God forgives us.

> "Therefore, the kingdom of heaven is like a king who wanted to settle accounts with his servants. As he began the settlement, a man who owed him ten thousand talents was brought to him. Since he was not able to pay, the master ordered that he and his wife and his children and all that he had be sold to repay the debt.
>
> "The servant fell on his knees before him. 'Be patient with me,' he begged, 'and I will pay back everything.' The servant's master took pity on him, canceled the debt and let him go.
>
> "But when that servant went out, he found one of his fellow servants who owed him a hundred denarii. He grabbed him and began to choke him. 'Pay back what you owe me!' he demanded.
>
> "His fellow servant fell to his knees and begged him, 'Be patient with me, and I will pay you back.'
>
> "But he refused. Instead, he went off and had the man thrown into prison until he could pay the debt. When the other servants saw what had happened, they were greatly distressed and went and told their master everything that had happened.
>
> "Then the master called the servant in. 'You wicked servant,' he said, 'I canceled all that debt of yours because you begged me to. Shouldn't you have had mercy on your fellow servant just as I had on you?' In anger his master turned him over to the jailers until he should pay back all he owed.
>
> "This is how my heavenly Father will treat each of you unless you forgive your brother from your heart." (Matthew 18:23–35)

Forgiven

This "once upon a time" parable begins with a powerful king and an indebted servant. Apparently the king was tightening up the finances of his realm by paying off his debts and collecting from his debtors. One of the king's servants owed him an enormous amount of money. The amount is so large that Jesus must have been using hyperbole in this parable to make a big point.

The debt was 10,000 talents. Talents were both a measure of money and weight. It is difficult to estimate how much money this would be in our dollars. It's hard enough for us to figure out the money equivalency in our own country and economy after only a decade of inflation. For example, a Kenmore microwave oven that cost $545 in 1980 cost $145 in 1994. The dollars were worth more in 1980, but the oven cost less in 1994. If something that recent from our own culture is hard to figure out, it's close to impossible to translate first-century talents into our twentieth-century dollars. But let's try to at least get an idea of how much money 10,000 talents was.

According to William Barclay's commentary on Matthew, the total revenue for the Roman province covering Idumaea, Judea, and Samaria was 600 talents. The total revenue for the province of Galilee was 300 talents. This means that the 10,000-talent debt was more than ten times the income of entire Roman provinces. Comparing that to today, it would be more than ten times the income of all the states west of the Rocky Mountains or ten times all the income of New England.

Obviously this servant had a major financial problem. No one could pay his debt. Not even the king himself could have paid it off.

The king figured he would get what he could by selling the man and his family into slavery. While it wouldn't produce much cash, it would be a warning for all his other debtors to pay up.

When he heard the king's ultimatum, the servant hit the floor. On his knees he began to beg, "Be patient with me and I will pay back everything!" His promise was wildly optimistic. The servant probably couldn't even have kept up with the interest on that much debt. There was no way he could ever pay back 10,000 talents.

But the king had pity on the man. Even though the debtor had done nothing to deserve it and even though the king would incur a tremendous loss, he forgave the debt. He went all the way. He didn't offer a 50,000-year payment schedule. He just canceled the note. In effect, he gave his employee a billion-dollar gift.

The servant must have felt great. Better than winning the Publisher's Clearinghouse Sweepstakes. It was the happiest moment of his life. He went in a debtor and came out debt free. Disaster turned to delight. Slavery became freedom. It was absolutely wonderful.

You know what Jesus was driving at. He was talking about us and God and sin. Jesus was saying our sins are so many, we are in a hole so deep, that we can never get ourselves out. Try to turn sin into numbers. How many do you think the average person commits?

There are sins of "commission" when we do something we shouldn't do. There are sins of "omission" when we don't do things that we should do. A grand total would have to include every sinful thought and word. Jesus said that each of us "will have to give account on the day of judgment for every careless word [we] have spoken" (Matthew 12:36). The total could be hundreds of sins per day.

If we estimated an average of 100 sins a day, we would reach 36,500 sins per year. By age ten a person is already up to 365,000 sins. At thirty years old the total is 1,095,000. Those who live to age eighty tally almost 3,000,000 sins.

Yet God will forgive them all. Those who come to Him, confessing those sins and asking for forgiveness, accepting Jesus Christ as Savior and Lord, are . . . forgiven! When Jesus died on the cross for our sins, He wiped out our incredible debt. All we must do is tell God we trust Him and accept His forgiveness. That acknowledges our debt is bigger than the parable talents, makes God a more merciful master than the parable king, and gives us far more forgiveness than the parable servant received.

Forgive

The forgiven servant came floating out of the king's palace, the happiest and most forgiven man in the kingdom. As he walked across the palace grounds, he ran into a fellow employee who owed him 100 denarii, which was about 100 days' wages for a laborer. Any amount of money is a lot if you don't have it, but compared to 10,000 talents, 100 denarii was very little. The coins for 100 denarii would fit in a man's pocket; the coins for 10,000 talents would fill a freight train. One analysis estimates that the second servant owed to the first servant only $\frac{1}{20,000}$ of 1% of what the first servant owed to the king. While it may have been a legal debt, it was virtually nothing compared to what had just been forgiven in the king's palace.

But the forgiven servant showed no mercy. He grabbed his co-worker by the throat and demanded that he immediately pay back his entire debt. When the forgiven servant heard the same plea he himself had just spoken to the king, he was not moved to compassion.

What should have happened is obvious. The big-debt-servant should have said to the little-debt-servant, "As I have been forgiven, so I forgive you. Be as free and happy as I am." Instead, "he went off and had the man thrown into prison until he could pay the debt." This sentence was made even more horrible by the fact that imprisoned debtors were tortured to reveal their secret hiding places for money so that debts could be paid.

The first servant was a rotten man. Had he so soon forgotten how much he had been forgiven? Did he not see himself in the plight of the other man? Could anyone be that selfish, greedy, and unforgiving?

Jesus told the story for our benefit. We who have been forgiven all our sins are to forgive others "seventy-seven times"—or, as many Bible scholars believe, "times without number." There is no injustice against us that outweighs the sins God has forgiven us, and God expects those He has forgiven to forgive others. To God this is serious business: "This is how my heavenly Father will treat each of you unless you forgive your brother from your heart."

The Rewards of Forgiveness

Forgiveness is not totally sacrificial. There are benefits to the person who does the forgiving.

"It takes a lot of emotional and psychological energy to keep a wound open, to keep a grudge alive," says Albert Haase, a Franciscan priest based in Taiwan who gives seminars and workshops on spirituality across the United States. "The longer I allow a wound to fester, the more bitterness, anger and self-pity poison my blood and eat at my heart."[1]

Holding on to hate and the desire to get even can do more damage than the original offense.

The Terrible Prayer

"Forgive our debts as we forgive our debtors." St. Augustine described that line in the Lord's Prayer as "the terrible petition." Praying this petition without forgiving others equals a plea for God *not* to forgive our sins.

James Edward Oglethorpe, founder and first governor of Georgia, proudly told a young British missionary, "I never forgive!" John Wesley replied, "Then, Sir, I hope you never sin."

There is no virtue more central to the Christian life than forgiveness. There is no practice more necessary for Christian living than forgiveness. Christians are those who have been forgiven by God and therefore must forgive others.

What If Forgiveness Is Not Asked?

A cassette tape of a sermon I had preached on forgiveness was sent to an American living overseas. He was not targeted by the tape or topic, it was simply part of a regular subscription service.

A few months later I received a strongly worded letter from the man telling me that what I taught on the tape was wrong. He insisted that there is never a need to forgive anyone who does not apologize and request forgiveness. The letter was so packed with emotion that I could read his personal story between the lines. He had been deeply wounded by someone who didn't care, wouldn't admit doing wrong, and would never apologize. It was too much for the offended Christian to forgive. He

---

[1]Martha Sawyer Allen, "The Art of Forgiveness Is a Thing to Give Thanks For," *Minneapolis Star Tribune* (November 21, 1993), 1B.

thought it would give greater power to the person who had hurt him and he wanted to continue his anger and resentment.

The basic meaning of forgiveness is "to let go." Forgiveness surrenders all claims for payment. Forgiveness keeps no record for purposes of revenge. Forgiveness releases ongoing resentment and bitterness. Forgiveness is always the responsibility of the offended.

Jesus said, "Father, forgive them," when He was being crucified. His executioners never apologized or asked to be forgiven. Yet Jesus forgave anyway, which is what He expects of His followers.

It is possible to get the impression from Scripture that forgiveness must be asked for before it is granted. For example, in Luke 17:3–4 Jesus says, "If your brother sins, rebuke him, and if he repents, forgive him. If he sins against you seven times in a day, and seven times comes back to you and says, 'I repent,' forgive him." These words require Christians to forgive when asked. However, they do not tell us not to forgive unless we are asked. To remove any confusion, Ephesians 4:31–32 adds the clarification that Christians must "get rid of all bitterness, rage and anger, brawling and slander, along with every form of malice. Be kind and compassionate to one another, forgiving each other, just as in Christ God forgave you." There is not a hint here of a required apology or request for forgiveness.

But wait a minute, you may be saying. Does all this mean that the child molester, heretic, or thief is automatically forgiven and allowed to immediately return to a place or position where he or she can sin all over again?

Restitution: Giving Back What Was Taken

Just as forgiveness is the responsibility of the offended, restitution is the responsibility of the offender. It is the offender's tangible expression of repentance and sincere effort to "make right" what has been done wrong.

Restitution is easiest to understand and perform in terms of property or money. It was spelled out for the Israelites in Numbers 5:5–7:

The LORD said to Moses, 'Say to the Israelites: "When a man or woman wrongs another in any way and so is unfaithful to the LORD, that person is guilty and must confess the sin he has committed. He must make full restitution for his wrong, add one fifth to it and give it all to the person he has wronged.' "

In extreme cases, the offender was required to give back five times as much as he stole (Exodus 22:1–5).

Luke 19:1–10 tells the story of Zacchaeus, the tax collector who gave half of his fortune to those he had cheated, repaying them four times as much as he had taken.

Restitution becomes more difficult to calibrate when the offense is gossip, incest, heresy, adultery, or discrimination. However, the principle is not altered simply because the repayment is harder to figure out. Restitution may include a formal apology to the offended person, correction of information to everyone involved, repair of property, writing a letter to set matters straight, paying for the counseling fees of the one who was hurt, or even serving a prison sentence. The purpose of restitution is to make every effort to put things back the way they were before the harm was done or to compensate for the wrong as much as is humanly possible.

Keeping the requirements for forgiveness and restoration separate is essential. Forgiveness is the responsibility and choice of the offended; restitution is the responsibility and choice of the offender. The Christian who was sinned against forgives whether or not there is repentance, apology, or efforts at restitution. The Christian who sinned should repent and make every effort at restitution whether forgiven or not.

Examples of both are evident in the attitudes and actions of Sandy and Doug. When Sandy needed a job, Doug hired her as a sales representative for White Birch Industries. Later the external auditors discovered that Sandy had cheated the company out of $4,500 through fraudulent expense account claims. In keeping with company policy, Doug confronted and fired Sandy. He did not report her to the police.

Both Doug and Sandy were Christians and active members of the same church. Out of Christian conviction, Doug decided to forgive Sandy, whether or not she apologized or repaid the money. This was not easy for him to do, however, for he felt hurt and angry. The greatest hurt for Doug was not the money lost but the betrayal and humiliation. He had helped Sandy when she needed employment, and he was embarrassed because other employees knew both were Christians and members of the same church. Hard as it was, though, Doug told Sandy that he forgave her and held no bitterness or resentment toward her.

Also out of Christian conviction, Sandy confessed her wrong to Doug, to several employees at White Birch Industries, and to the leaders of her church. She voluntarily sold her car and several pieces of furniture in order to repay the $4,500 plus interest and expenses. This was not easy for Sandy because she was out of work and didn't have much money. Even harder was going to people she knew and humbly admitting what she had done and asking for their forgiveness. Restitution was something Sandy decided to do before she knew about Doug's forgiveness and without any expectation that she could possibly regain her old job.

Should Sandy get her job back? Do forgiveness and restitution require restoration?

Reinstatement: Returning to Former Position

Frequently there is confusion among Christians over the relationship between forgiveness and reinstatement, leading to a common conclusion: "If you really forgive a person, you will allow that person to return to his or her former position." The implication—and sometimes the direct accusation—is that lack of reinstatement really means lack of forgiveness. When this occurs, somehow the tables are turned and the offended becomes the offender, accused of great wrong for failing to reinstate the one whom she forgave for sinning against her.

In some situations reinstatement is right and in some situations it is wrong. But never does true forgiveness *require* full reinstatement to former privileges and responsibilities.

When God forgave human sin, He did not return Adam and Eve or their descendants to the Garden of Eden. King David sinned, confessed his sin, and was forgiven by God, but God did not release David from the full and permanent consequences of his sin. The prodigal son in Jesus' parable came home and confessed his sin and stupidity. His father lovingly forgave him and fully reinstated him to his previous standing (much to the dismay of the prodigal's brother). Different situations require different approaches.

Galatians 6:1 is subject to some misunderstanding because of the way it was translated in the King James Version of the Bible: "Brethren, if a man be overtaken in a fault, ye which are spiritual, restore such an one in the spirit of meekness; considering thyself, lest thou also be tempted." The "fault" here is more in the category of a mistake than an intentional sin, and "restore" does not mean reinstatement but "setting right." *The New English Bible* more accurately captures the intended sense with its translation: "If a man should do something wrong, my brothers, on a sudden impulse, you who are endowed with the Spirit must set him right again very gently."

The best way to set a person right may be to keep him or her away from a former position. The social worker who is continually tempted to abuse children is not helped by reinstatement to his old job as resident counselor in a children's group home. The flight attendant who was fired for stealing alcohol from the plane's galley may not have her attraction to alcohol helped by returning to the skies. The preacher whose prominent position led to pride, which triggered immorality, false teaching, and misuse of funds, may be far better off never pastoring again.

Reinstatement affects more than the offender. The church gossip who shattered reputations may be forgiven and cured, but for the sake of the church and the trust of parishioners should perhaps be restricted from access to confidential information. The physician who lost her license for writing illegal prescriptions may never practice medicine again to protect the integrity of her former profession. The politician who betrayed a public trust may be fully forgiven but never reelected because return to office might diminish the overall effectiveness of the government.

Biblical examples of no reinstatement include Adam and

Eve's permanent removal from the Garden of Eden, King Saul's permanent loss of Israel's throne, and the interesting law of Deuteronomy 24:4 that a divorced wife who remarries may never be restored to her former husband.

Fortunately, there are many biblical examples of those who were restored. Samson lost his strength but got it back again (Judges 13–16). King Nebuchadnezzar returned to the throne of Babylon (Daniel 4). The eleven disciples who abandoned Jesus before His crucifixion were not only restored but promoted to become apostles. John Mark, who deserted Paul and Barnabas on their missionary travels, later rejoined Paul's missionary team (Acts 13; Colossians 4:10).

It is wrong to establish legalistic and arbitrary rules that are supposed to fit every person and situation. That may be an easy way, but it is not the best way. Different circumstances require different responses.

Dave Carder, in his book *Secrets of Your Family Tree*, addresses the moral failure of pastors. In doing so, he distinguishes between Type I (the "one night stand"), Type II (long-term friendship that leads to an ongoing extramarital affair), and Type III (promiscuous sexual addiction with multiple sexual partners). While citing biblical examples for each, Carder explains that Type I may be restored to ministry after repentance, Type II requires repentance and long-term help for healing and correction, and Type III should probably never again hold the office of pastor.[2]

Before a Christian leader is restored to a previously held position—if that is the appropriate course—the offender should have ample opportunity to establish a new track record. In some cases this will take a relatively short time, but often it will take years. Qualification for church leadership includes current evidence of Christian character, including being a one-wife kind of man (1 Timothy 3:2) and not a drunkard (1 Timothy 3:3). The qualifications for elders and deacons in 1 Timothy 3 take into account present behavior, not past history. Many first-century Christians would not have made it into church leadership

---

[2]Dave Carder, "Patterns Predicting Pastoral Infidelity" (Appendix B), *Secrets of Your Family Tree* (Chicago: Moody Press, 1991), 287–289.

if they had been judged on the basis of past sins.

Christianity is a religion of grace and growth that values the principle "always forgive and always try to restore." In the spirit of forgiveness, the Christian community hopes for and looks for God's grace in a person's life. We never restrict or limit what God can do to transform someone for good.

When all the pieces come together, we—and the world—see a beautiful demonstration of Christian community. Forgiveness, restitution, and reinstatement restore former relationships fractured by sin. The grace and power of God overrule the devastation of human sin. God is glorified and Christians are Christlike.

Questions

For Thought:

1. The basic meaning of forgiveness is to "let go." What are some ways in your life that you can let go and forgive?
2. When someone sins against you, what is your first response? Do you forgive, hold a grudge, sin back in anger or retaliation? Reread Jesus' parable in Matthew 18:23–35 and think about what it means to forgive "from your heart."

For Discussion:

1. What are some of the benefits to the person forgiving and to the person who is forgiven?
2. What are some of the consequences of not forgiving someone? (Spiritually, psychologically, physically, etc.)
3. Being reinstated to a position depends on credibility, restitution, repentance, wisdom, and many other issues. Discuss how wisdom plays an important role in this issue.
4. Should we forgive someone if they have not asked for forgiveness? Why or why not?

Chapter 12

Making More Disciples

THE ABBOT of the monastery called the young novice into his chambers and told him he was to present the homily at the next morning's chapel. The novice pleaded to be released from the assignment, saying he was too frightened and inadequate to speak to all of the brothers in the monastery. The more he pleaded, however, the more the abbot was convinced that the novice needed to fulfill the assignment.

Early the next morning, the novice stood at the chapel pulpit, his knees knocking together and his hands shaking. His voice was silent from fear. All of the brothers sat in quiet anticipation. The abbot sat in quiet frustration.

At last the frightened novice spoke: "Do you know what I'm going to say?" The brothers shook their heads back and forth. Then the novice said, "Neither do I. Let us stand for the benediction. Pax vobiscum."

The abbot was angry. He ordered the frightened young man to give the homily in the next day's chapel.

The next morning the whole scene was repeated. Fear. Trembling. Silence. When he finally spoke, he said, "Do you know what I'm going to say?" This time all the brothers nodded their heads up and down. "Then there is no need for me to tell you," said the novice. "Let us stand for the benediction. Pax vobiscum."

By now the abbot was furious. He warned the novice that this had better not happen again or he would be on bread and water in an isolation cell for a month. Tomorrow he would speak . . . or else!

On the third morning, as the novice stepped to the pulpit, tension mounted in the usually peaceful chapel. After a long pause, he asked, "Do you know what I'm going to say?" Half the heads nodded yes and half shook their heads no. "Then," said the young man, "let those who know tell those who don't! Let us stand for the benediction. Pax vobiscum."

Well, the poor young novice wound up on bread and water. He also gave us the simplest definition of evangelism: "Those who know telling those who don't."

But the simplest definition is not an adequate definition. To be fully biblical, we must define evangelism as "making more disciples for Jesus Christ."

Doing Evangelism

Evangelism begins with the Good News. The Greek word for evangelism is *euangelion*. *Eu* means "good" and *angelion* means "message." The pieces add up to "good message." Another English word that means the same is "gospel." The Gospel of Jesus Christ is the "evangel" of Jesus Christ, the Good News.

Interestingly, the word "evangelism" is never used in the New Testament the way most people use it today. To many Christians, evangelism means telling about Jesus, about salvation, either by preaching or witnessing. But that was never "it" in the Bible. Telling about Jesus only begins evangelism.

Suppose someone asks you how to get from Cleveland to Chicago and you say, "Get into your car." Good answer, but hardly complete.

Evangelism begins with information about Jesus Christ as Savior and Lord, but there is much more. Evangelism includes persuading someone to become a disciple of Jesus Christ. In Matthew 28:19–20 Jesus defines evangelism when He says, "Therefore go and make disciples of all nations, baptizing them in the name of the Father and of the Son and of the Holy Spirit, and teaching them to obey everything I have commanded you." Evangelism is convincing another person to commit his or her life to Jesus Christ and to obey Him. This goes far beyond telling. Evangelism requires persuasion and commitment.

A salesperson is someone who not only talks about a product but closes the sale. A sale is not a sale until a customer signs the contract, pays the price, and takes delivery.

An evangelist is a person who talks about Jesus and His Good News *and* closes the sale. Evangelism is not evangelism until someone accepts Jesus Christ as Savior, agrees to obey whatever Jesus asks, and takes delivery of Jesus Christ as Lord of life.

Some distinguish between evangelism and discipleship by comparing them to obstetrics and pediatrics: one involves birthing a child and the other deals with raising a child. But you will find no such distinction between evangelism and discipleship in the Bible. As far as God is concerned, evangelism and discipleship are the same thing—making more disciples for Jesus Christ.

The Great Commission was one of Jesus' final statements before He returned to heaven. It summarizes the anticipated expansion of what Jesus had begun in His life and ministry on earth.

To adequately understand what Jesus asked requires a quick analysis of the Greek grammar in Matthew 28:19–20. Many English translations quote Jesus as ordering Christians to "go," but the word in the original language is a participle, not an imperative verb. A better translation is "going." Jesus assumed that Christians would spread out all over the world and that as they were going they should "make disciples." The only command in the Great Commission is to make disciples. All the other verb forms explain how to do it: by going, baptizing, and teaching.

What Jesus anticipated actually happened. The few Christians He left moved from Jerusalem to Judea, Samaria, and the rest of the world and multiplied by thousands in the process

(Acts 1:8). Some of those moves were involuntary because of persecution (Acts 8:1). Everywhere these Christians went they encountered those who had never heard of Christ or who did not believe in Him. Their job was to tell the Good News, persuade the non-Christians to become Christians, baptize them as a mark of conversion, and then teach them. All this was part of the disciple-making process.

It is important to note that Jesus did *not* tell His followers to "teach them all I have commanded you." That would have put the emphasis on content. Jesus emphasized obedience. He told them to "teach them to *obey* everything I have commanded you." The difference is neither subtle nor unimportant. It is at the very heart of what evangelism and discipleship are all about. A person who learns the words of Jesus without obedience becomes an educated individual whose life is unchanged. On the other hand, a new Christian who learns to obey whatever Jesus commanded is motivated to learn Jesus' words. It takes a lifetime to learn all Jesus wants us to do, but it takes a single act of the will to become an obedient disciple.

Evangelism is the process of moving an uninformed non-Christian to an understanding of the Good News—faith in Jesus Christ as Savior—and commitment to obey Jesus as boss. If a practical distinction needs to be made between evangelism and discipleship, think of them as a whole process of *disciple making*, with evangelism being the introductory phase from ignorance and unbelief to knowledge, commitment, and obedience.

Once a person is evangelized, he or she should automatically evangelize others because "making disciples" is a clear command of Jesus.

Why Evangelize?

We don't evangelize for ourselves. We don't evangelize for the church. In a sense, we don't even evangelize for the people we persuade to become Christians. We evangelize for Jesus Christ.

Think in terms of primary and secondary motives for evangelism. The primary motive must be Jesus himself: obedience to what He says and gratitude for what He has done. Secondary motives include love for people, a longing for them to be saved from sin and its consequences, and a desire for them to become Christians with all the benefits of belonging to God.

Missionaries have gone to every part of the world to fulfill the Great Commission. In South Korea, South America, parts of Indonesia and sub-Sahara Africa the results have been counted in millions of new Christians. But missionaries to North Africa, the Middle East, and other parts of Muslim Indonesia have seen few if any conversions. Does this mean that some missionaries are better motivated or more successful, based on the results? No, motivation or "success" is not measured by numbers. Of course, there is great joy when large numbers believe, just as there is sadness when nobody believes. But faithful missionaries are motivated by obedience to Jesus, not by the final count.

This principle also applies to Christians who stay home. We are called to obey Jesus' command to evangelism just as much as any missionary. We want our neighbors, co-workers, friends, and relatives to believe. But our measure of success is in the obedience, not just the results.

Evangelism often leads to a clear clash of values between Christians and non-Christians. In many countries it is legal to be a Christian but not to evangelize. In Muslim, Hindu, and Buddhist cultures it may be a crime for a Christian to seek to persuade a non-Christian to become a disciple of Jesus Christ. Sometimes it is a capital offense to evangelize, and Christians who do are executed.

The People's Republic of China distinguishes between the state-recognized church (called the Three Self Church because it is self-contained and not controlled by religious hierarchies outside of China) and the unregistered "house churches" (called this because they often meet in homes). I have attended a Three Self Church worship service. The Bible was taught, familiar Christian hymns were sung, and the people appeared to be free to believe in Jesus. But they are not free to evangelize.

The Three Self churches don't usually grow because there is no way to recruit new Christians. The house churches aggressively evangelize, even though it is against the law, and their numbers are growing by the millions. Conservative estimates count more than fifty million believers in China. Most Chinese Christians in the house churches say that if a person does not evangelize, that person is not a Christian. Despite large numbers of imprisonments and executions they keep on evangelizing and multiplying. Nothing stops them.

In spite of our freedom to evangelize without fear here in the West, many do not value evangelism. Just try the word "evangelism" on a few co-workers and see how quickly they attach negative value to the term. I once watched a focus group of non-Christians critique the literature of a local church. They liked the lines about loving and helping people but strongly reacted against the church's commitment to evangelism. Evangelism was considered inappropriate, an invasion of privacy.

Evangelism makes no sense to non-Christians. "Believe whatever you want to believe," many say with a shrug, "just keep it to yourself. Religion is a private thing. Leave other people alone. Other religions are just as good as yours. Back off. Who do you think you are anyway?"

Popular American culture increasingly values tolerance, privacy, and individualism. The idea of one person trying to persuade another person to change religious beliefs runs counter to these values.

Christians, however, have a very different set of values from non-Christians, and one of the sharpest points of difference is evangelism. The Bible convinces us that a personal relationship with God through Jesus Christ is more valuable than tolerance, privacy, or individualism. This is not to say that Christians should pursue a theocracy (Christian government) or use force to make disciples. To the contrary, we have a long historical commitment to freedom of religion that allows ideas and faiths to compete. We believe that Christian truth is both powerful and persuasive in an atmosphere of openness and freedom. Christians really want to *persuade* unbelievers to become disciples, never to coerce them.

God places high value on evangelism. He gave His Son's life for the Good News, and He has commissioned every Christian to join in making disciples. And what is valuable to God is valuable to Christians. The number one reason we persuade people to believe—the number one reason we send missionaries—

is to please God. We evangelize for God's sake even more than for the sake of the people we seek to persuade.

All Christians have been evangelized. Someone told us. Someone persuaded us. Someone taught us how to follow and obey Jesus. We are Christians because we've been on the receiving end of evangelism. Since we've been evangelized, since we've been forgiven of every sin, since we have a personal relationship with Jesus Christ, since we're headed to heaven, we know how good it is. And we want others to get in on what we've discovered.

What convinces people to buy cars or books or soft drinks? Sure, advertising helps. But the greatest persuader is a satisfied customer. Those who are the greatest beneficiaries of something good are the best salespersons.

John Grisham became one of the top-selling fiction writers of the 1990s after the success of his second book, *The Firm*. His first book, *A Time to Kill*, had been sort of a flop, selling only 5,000 copies in first-run hardcover. His second book didn't receive great reviews or much publicity, but many who read it loved it, and *The Firm* quickly sold over seven million copies and was made into a movie starring Tom Cruise. Why? Because people who liked the book persuaded others to read it. The success of *The Firm* created interest in Grisham's other work, and *A Time to Kill* was republished. It also became a best seller. Word-of-mouth promotion can't be bought for any price. And it can't be stopped.

Why do Christians value evangelism? Because we love Jesus Christ and we want to tell others about Him. We've experienced what He can do for those who become Christians. So we evangelize.

I recently had lunch with a man who told me story after story of people he had introduced to Jesus Christ and who had become disciples. He said, "I still remember what it was like not to be a Christian." In business terminology, he was a satisfied customer. He remembered the guilt of unforgiven sin, the hopelessness of life, the lack of connection with God, the absence of answered prayer, and the daily grind of life without Christian joy. Now he has what he lacked, and he tells everyone who will listen.

Christians also value evangelism for the sake of others. We don't want anyone to be lost from God. We want them to have their sins forgiven. We want them to receive God into their lives. We want them to experience the peace and joy and all the good that comes to those who are disciples of Jesus Christ.

Maybe you've seen the T-shirts that say "Friends Don't Let Friends Go to Hell." You may not want to wear one of those shirts to work, but you get the idea. Christians really care about other people, and we want the best for our family, friends, neighbors, and co-workers. And the best they can get is Jesus. We take very seriously the sobering words of Jesus in John 3:36: "Whoever believes in the Son has eternal life, but whoever rejects the Son will not see life, for God's wrath remains on him."

When I was a nineteen-year-old college student, I met a middle-aged man whom I have never forgotten, even though our meeting lasted less than an hour. It was a hot spring evening in Chicago. As we talked, I explained to him that I was a Christian, and I encouraged him to become a Christian. He then told me his story. When he was in his early twenties, he had murdered a man. He was arrested, tried, convicted, and sentenced. Only months before our conversation he had been paroled. It became increasingly obvious that I was not the first person to talk to him about becoming a Christian and that he had given God a great deal of thought. With a profound sadness he told me that God would never forgive the sin of murder and that he could not become a Christian. I tried everything I could think of to persuade him that God will forgive murder, that God has forgiven murderers, and that Jesus Christ died with and for murderers. I just couldn't persuade him. My heart was heavy for him then and is heavy for him now, because I realize how bad life is for that man and how good it could be if he would believe. I hope he has done so.

Another spring day several years later I received a telephone call from an emergency room nurse asking me to rush over to the hospital. There had been a terrible construction accident. A crane had fallen over and crushed the operator's chest. Hospital personnel were fighting to save his life, preparing him for surgery, but offering little hope for his survival. When I arrived, only a few minutes remained before the operation. The man was conscious and his eyes were filled with panic. I admit that I was uncomfortable trying to evangelize someone I had just met while surrounded by eight physicians and nurses who were working on him. Because of the apparatus in his mouth there was no way for him to respond except to move his head slightly. "Buck, you must know that this is really serious," I said, connecting with his eyes. "They are going to do everything possible to save your life, and I'm praying for God's help for you. Now I need to talk to you about God and I don't have much time, so please listen. God loves you. He sent His Son Jesus to become a man like us and to die on the cross to pay for our sin. If we ask God, He will forgive all our sin and guarantee us eternal life in heaven when we die. To do this you must believe that Jesus died for you and completely give your life to Him forever. Do you think you understand?" He indicated with his eyes and a slight head movement that he understood. "Buck, I know you can't talk out loud, but God can hear you. So tell Him right now that you believe in Jesus and want your sins forgiven and want to become a Christian. Will you do that?" Again he indicated, "Yes."

I left the room and Buck was rolled out for hours of surgery. When I had spoken to the surgeon, he had told me he didn't have high hopes for Buck's survival. He said he had operated on a number of "crush victims" in Vietnam and the damage was usually too great to repair. If Buck did live, he would probably be paralyzed for the rest of his life.

I can't adequately describe my feelings during those next hours. Frankly, I had felt a little foolish talking to a dying patient and trying to summarize Christianity in so few words while the medical experts surrounded him. I felt like I was in the way. I wondered what the doctors and nurses thought of me. Besides, I really wasn't sure he even heard or understood me. Maybe the look in his eyes and the shake of his head was more my imagination than his response. Still, while I wasn't sure I had done it very well, I was convinced that I had done the right thing.

Buck survived the surgery. His life teetered near death for days afterward, then he slowly started to improve. When he was well enough to be moved, he was transferred to another hospital and later moved to a long-term rehabilitation facility where he met a Christian nurse. The rest of the story was relayed back to me through the nurse's co-worker. He told the nurse of his commitment to Christ before surgery and she gave him a Bible to read. She reported his strong spiritual growth amid minimal recovery from extensive paralysis. Truly, Buck was evangelized.

In light of that, everything else rather pales in comparison, doesn't it? Which was more important, what the physicians and nurses thought or what God thought? Which was more valuable, the saving of Buck's body or the saving of his soul?

What to Do?

Some of you may be asking, "But what should I do? I am a Christian, and I *do* value evangelism, but I don't know how to do it." Some simple suggestions:

Pray. Before you do anything else, ask God to help you learn and give you opportunity. Try praying every day for three people you would like to evangelize. Worry later about how to do it. Just pray for them, for their needs, and that they will become Christians. Pray for them daily, week after week, month after month. If appropriate, ask them what you could pray about for them.

Consider making a covenant with other Christians to pray together. Those who pray corporately, in addition to praying individually, usually stay with the prayer plan longer, pray with greater faith, and experience the compounding of spiritual power.

Body evangelism. This occurs when members of the body of Christ (the church) work together to evangelize instead of expecting everyone to evangelize individually. Spiritual teamwork works to win others.

Body evangelism is rooted in a basic understanding that the Great Commission (Matthew 28:19–20) is not spoken to us only as individual Christians but to all of us together as the body of Christ, the church. There is no way that individuals just working on their own could "make disciples of all nations."

By the way, those "nations" are not political governments, such as those belonging to the United Nations. "Nations" refers to the ethnic "people groups" of the world. For example, there are many people groups in North America, including Hispanics, Native Americans, French-speaking Canadians, along with English-speaking Anglos.

Around the world there are thousands of people groups, ranging from a few hundred in size to millions. The expectation of Jesus Christ is for Christians to work together to make disciples and establish the church in each of these groups.

Just as teamwork is necessary on a global scale it is effective on a local level. Think of it in terms of one local church with 245 members. Bob drives the same route to work every day and often picks up hitchhikers or offers rides to co-workers. One day he gives a ride to Bill and they become friends. Bill comes along with Bob to a church softball game and meets Herb and Heather, who invite Bill to their home Bible study on Tuesday nights. The study is team-taught by the Carlsons, who explain the gospel to Bill for the first time during one of the group sessions. He thinks about it for a long time and finally, one Tuesday night during their break for refreshments, tells Kathy that he just doesn't get it. She not only answers his questions and clarifies what it means to be a Christian, but persuades him to pray a prayer in the car on the way home, accepting Jesus Christ as his Savior and Lord. Wednesday morning Bob gives Bill a ride and Bill shares the good news that he became a Christian the night before. Bob knows that Bill needs some personal follow-up, so he connects Bill with Gary Klein, who agrees to be Bill's spiritual mentor for the next six months. During those six months Gary invites Bill to church, where he makes more friends, is baptized, and continues to mature. This is an example of body evangelism: the whole body working together to take a man from spiritual ignorance to Christian discipleship.

Body evangelism is a New Testament concept based not only on the intent of Matthew 28:19–20, but also on the spiritual gift theology of 1 Corinthians 12–14.

An important distinction between "witness" and "evangelist" helps make body evangelism work. Ephesians 4:11 says that only some Christians are evangelists: "It was he who gave some to be apostles, some to be prophets, some to be evangelists. . . ." They are the ones like Kathy who are especially gifted in "closing" the decision to believe. Not everyone is equally gifted at evangelism, so God does not expect us all to do what Kathy does. However, we are all expected to be witnesses: "But you will receive power when the Holy Spirit comes on you; and you will be my witnesses . . ." (Acts 1:8). We are all expected to tell others what we have experienced and about the impact Jesus Christ has had on our lives. When every Christian responsibly witnesses, it is like spreading millions of seeds. Other Christians will help water, weed, and nurture those seeds so that the evangelists can later come through and harvest them.

One of the wonderful results of body evangelism is that the credit does not go to any individual but to God who coordinates the ministry of all Christians in the church.

Make friends. Friendship is an increasingly effective means of evangelism. One of the growing changes in North American culture is the way people come into relationships with Christ and the church. Less than a generation ago people tended to come to a church, become Christians, and then make friends. Today it is much more likely that people will first make friends outside of the church and then come to Christ and the church because of the friendship. The reasons for this are multiple: less trust of institutional religion, greater loneliness and desire for friendships, and deciding major issues of life less on the basis of reason and more on the basis of relationships.

If Christians don't befriend others, someone else will; and the chances are good that the beliefs and values of that someone else will be adopted. The more friends Christians make among non-Christians, the more effective evangelism becomes. Today fewer people are talked into Christianity and more people are befriended into Christianity.

Learn. Buy a book on how to evangelize, or take a training seminar. Excellent materials are available. Perhaps the best practical advice is to find another Christian who has a heart for evangelism and has had experience with evangelism and ask to be taught. After all, how-to books and seminars are relatively recent inventions compared to the old-fashioned way of one Christian learning from another Christian.

No doubt the best way to learn is by doing. I remember a time when I was very uncomfortable with evangelism. I had read books and taken classes, but I never did evangelism unless it was forced on me. Like the time when I was a camp counselor and a boy asked me how to become a Christian. I stumbled my way through an explanation, but other than that my experience was minimal. Then I read an early edition of *Evangelism Explosion* by D. James Kennedy.[1] In fact, I read it several times to learn the approach to evangelism he outlines. Then I resolved to try it with a couple who lived a few blocks from our house. I was anything but smooth. When I came to the point of asking the couple to become Christians, I lost my courage and went home. Ashamed of my cowardice, I returned the next Saturday morning and asked if they had thought about what I had told them. They said they had and both wanted to accept Jesus Christ. That positive experience gave me the encouragement to try with others until I became more comfortable and confident in evangelism.

Let those who know tell those who don't. Pax vobiscum.

Questions

For Thought:

1. What does it mean to "make a disciple" of Jesus Christ?
2. Why should you as a Christian have a desire in your heart to tell others about Jesus Christ and help them enter into faith?
3. If you feel afraid about doing evangelism, what steps could you take to overcome your fear? (Attend a seminar, go with someone who is already experienced in evangelism, etc.)

For Discussion:

1. Talk about the primary and secondary reasons for evangelizing.
2. What are some steps you can take right now to learn more about evangelism and become involved?

---

[1]D. James Kennedy, *Evangelism Explosion*, new edition (Wheaton, Ill.: Tyndale House Publishers, 1983).

Chapter 13

The Forgotten Value

BOB LAMSE was an elder of Wooddale Church in the 1970s. He owned and operated Carousel Porsche-Audi in suburban Minneapolis until he sold the business and moved to Georgia and then to Florida. In 1990 he was diagnosed with cancer that eventually took his life. Shortly after the initial diagnosis he underwent major surgery in south Florida. I was there to see him before the operation and waited until he was brought from the recovery room.

As I stood by his bed, it was obvious that Bob was in great pain in spite of the medical efforts to make him comfortable. He asked me to come closer. I bent over, and through the pain he whispered words into my ear that I will never forget. He said, "Leith, it is such an honor for me to experience just a little bit of the kind of suffering which I know Jesus experienced for me on the cross."

In the midst of his anguish, Bob Lamse acknowledged the forgotten value of Christianity—suffering. My heart was heavy for my friend and what he was going through, but my soul was truly touched by the profound discovery of truth Bob declared in his darkest hour.

We live at a time when people become Christians for the sake of happiness. We tend to place high value on ourselves and our comforts. We like everything to be as pleasant and perfect as possible. I see it in myself. I like the weather to be perfect on the outside and the temperature comfortable on the inside; I want good health and good friends and good times.

Many today even go so far as to believe that true Christians never suffer. What a difference from the followers of Jesus Christ in earlier centuries who believed that suffering was a necessary part of the Christian life and an evidence of true faith.

A biblical characteristic of Christianity that makes it a unique religion is the way Christians face and value suffering. What other religion would dare say, "Consider it pure joy . . . whenever you face trials of many kinds" (James 1:2)?

Sources of Suffering

Not all suffering is the same. The Bible lists many different sources of suffering. Determining the source goes a long way toward our response.

Sin

When human sin was born in the Garden of Eden, God clearly explained that sin always brings suffering (Genesis 3:16–19). Adam and Eve made a tragic choice against God and for sin. It was like releasing a highly contagious virus that spread from person to person and generation to generation. With the epidemic of sin has come universal suffering and inevitable death.

That suffering began with the hard labor of childbirth and the hard labor of making a living. It scarred the environment and genetically altered humanity by making us all sinners. We all suffer directly and indirectly from sin.

The direct consequences of sin come because of what we have done. Immorality can destroy a marriage and bring a sexually transmitted disease. Violence can lead to criminal charges and legal consequences. Uncontrolled temper can damage relationships with those we love most. The list is long. We all sin and we all suffer as a direct result. Current culture minimizes the human responsibility and maximizes the suffering that has turned millions of Americans into self-declared victims. The truth is that much of our suffering is self-induced, whether we admit it or not. When suffering comes as a direct consequence of our sin, our response should be admission of guilt, confession to God, appropriate restitution, and acceptance of the consequences. As painful as all of this may be, suffering the direct consequences of sin can bring us to God as repentant sinners who would otherwise have continued in sin and kept God at a distance.

The indirect consequences of sin are everywhere, affect everyone, and are awful. Sin contaminated earth and humanity with communicable diseases, genetic defects, natural disasters, and the ability of evil to spread its effects upon innocent people. A drunken driver survives a crash that kills a busload of grade-school children. The bullets fired by an angry employee take the lives of a mail room full of postal employees. Children are born with AIDS. Bridges collapse. Fire from a single cigarette destroys an entire town. No one is exempt and no one is excluded. Everyone suffers from the indirect consequences of sin in our world. Perhaps the hardest part is that these consequences seem so senseless, often expressed by those who ask, "Why me?"

We cannot escape sin's consequences; what we can and must do is decide how we will respond. Some choose to bitterly turn against God for not exempting them from this indiscriminate suffering. Others recognize that it is part of life in a contaminated world and turn to God for comfort and help.

Discipline

A second source of suffering is discipline from God. Hebrews 12:6 gives us God's perspective on this, telling us that "the Lord disciplines those he loves."

To help us understand, God uses the analogy of human parenthood. Good parents discipline their children because they love them. Because God loves us—His children—He disciplines us, and that discipline often comes in the form of suffering. It is not intended to be punishment. It is intended only for correction. If we misbehave and God does not discipline us, that may indicate that we are not truly Christians.

"I'm going to leave my wife," the man told me. I couldn't believe it. This couple had been married for more than twenty years—happily so, I thought. When I asked why, he said, "I want a change. I want to find another woman." He wasn't leaving because his wife had done anything wrong or because there was another woman. He just wanted a change.

I told him this was a bad choice and called on him as a Christian to reconsider and return to his wife. Amazingly, he acknowledged that what he was going to do was wrong. But after he did it, he said, he would confess his sin to God and God would forgive him.

I thought about this man's situation and his solution for his sin for days before settling on what to tell him. He was right about God forgiving him, I concluded. In many ways I didn't like that conclusion. His plan to sin and then to take such manipulative advantage of God's grace seemed incredible. Yet the Bible teaches that when we confess our sins God is faithful to forgive them (1 John 1:9) and that there is no condemnation for those who are Christians (Romans 8:1). Some might doubt that a true disciple of Jesus Christ would plan and follow through on such direct defiance of God's will. But experience tells me that Christians are still capable of great sin and that God's grace can be classified as "outrageous" by human standards. Yes, I concluded, he could directly disobey God's will, confess his sin after the fact, and be forgiven.

But he also needed to hear about God's discipline. If he is a Christian and he deliberately sins, God promises He will discipline him because the Lord always disciplines those whom He loves (Hebrews 12:6). So, he should anticipate suffering to correct him and redirect him as an expression of God's love and commitment to him. On the other hand, if he proceeds with his plan and does not receive discipline from God, he should assume that he is not a Christian. Lack of suffering, of God's discipline in his life, would be a clear indication that he should immediately repent of all sin and accept Jesus Christ into his life in order to become a Christian.

Suffering Christians should ask, "God, is this suffering from you in order to discipline and correct me?" If there is sin, it should be stopped. Under such circumstances every Christian should be grateful for the suffering that proves God's love. If we can't figure out a connection between the suffering and some sin in our life, and if God does not answer our prayer-question, it is appropriate to conclude that our suffering is not intended as divine discipline for a particular sin.

Persecution

In His Sermon on the Mount, Jesus told of a third source of suffering: "Blessed are those who are persecuted because of righteousness . . ." (Matthew 5:10). A Christian will be treated the way Jesus was treated—and that included persecution.

Persecution is suffering because a person is identified with Jesus Christ and because a person does what is right. Some who are persecuted lose their jobs. Some are divorced for righteousness' sake. Millions have died in this century because they were Christians. In fact, there have been more martyrs for Jesus Christ in the twentieth century than in all of previous history combined.

Persecution can take many different forms. Both the Roman Empire in the early centuries and the Soviet Union in the twentieth century persecuted Christians by taking away their children. That can be a horror worse than physical torture and death. Christians have been ordered to deny their faith or their children will be tortured. Christians have been told to renounce Jesus Christ or their children will be taken away from them and raised as atheists.

In preparation for a visit to China I read some of the writings of Jonathan Chao, who is both a fine theologian and a Sinologist. I was somewhat dismayed to read that Christians in the People's Republic of China consider suffering for Christ an essential evidence of true faith. While visiting Dr. Chao in Taipei I asked him how this could be, because it would mean that there are very few true Christians in the United States or Canada. His answer was quick and significant. He said that our Chinese brothers and sisters in Christ would say that Christians in America suffer persecution in their marriages and families. If that is true, this generation's suffering has been great as divorces have become epidemic and prodigal children numerous.

The diagnosis of suffering because of persecution also begins with a prayer-question to God, asking Him if problems we face are a result of our faithfulness to our Lord. The pain is not less if this is true, but there is a realization that we are privileged to remain faithful when the cost is high.

Origin Unknown

Whenever a Christian suffers it is helpful to determine why. Am I a victim of another's sin? Is it because I have done wrong and God is disciplining me? Or am I being persecuted because I have done right?

And what if it is none of the above? Many Christians are like the Old Testament saint Job, who suffered severely and never knew why. When we read his famous biography, we learn that Job's troubles resulted because of an extraordinary debate between God and Satan (Job 1). When Satan claims there are no humans who love God and remain faithful to Him unless they get something good in return, God points to Job. That begins a forty-two-chapter biography of misery in which Satan systematically kills Job's children, steals his friends, and destroys his wealth, prestige, power, and health. Job's sufferings are legendary, but he never gives up on God. What is most amazing is often overlooked: Job never knew why he was suffering. God knew. Satan knew. We know. But Job never found out. There was a reason, but it was never made known to Job.

If we cannot pinpoint the source as sin, discipline, or persecution, then we must consider our suffering as of unknown origin. The Bible calls on Christians to do what seems impossible when we face such suffering: to rejoice (James 1:2)! Our joy is not in the pain but in the confidence that God uses such suffering to accomplish great good in our lives.

Think about it. Are not the most important lessons in life more often learned in pain than pleasure? Ask almost any

Christian when he or she most significantly experienced the power and presence of God. The vast majority will say it was when suffering from a broken relationship, deep disappointment, physical illness, or other pain. I've not heard of people learning the greatest lessons of life and coming closest to God when winning the lottery or sleeping late on a day off.

Even unknown suffering can have its positive purpose.

Values of Suffering

Christians dare to go beyond endurance of suffering to actually value suffering. We can see and experience good in the pain that others passionately avoid.

Sharing the Experience of Jesus

The value of sharing the suffering experience of Jesus is one of the most wonderful and unusual values of the Christian life. It is what Bob Lamse talked about from his hospital bed. Romans 8:17 explains that "if we are children, then we are heirs—heirs of God and co-heirs with Christ, if indeed we share in his sufferings in order that we may also share in his glory."

There is a solidarity of suffering that brings and binds people together like little else. It is the comradeship of men and women who have experienced war or cancer or unemployment or the death of a loved one.

If I talk about a suffering I have never experienced, those who have suffered immediately can tell. No matter how graphically I describe the pain of cancer or the disappointment of a divorce, they know I speak from observation, not from personal experience. If I share my own suffering, I may stumble in my description of losing a job or the death of my father, but any who have traveled those roads know I have traveled them too.

Jesus suffered for us. We can never fully know the horror of His acceptance of human sin and the consequence of death by crucifixion. But those who suffer great pain connect with Jesus in a way that others cannot.

The value is not in the suffering but in what the suffering does: It makes us one with Jesus.

Anticipating the Future

Romans 8:18 says that "our present sufferings are not worth comparing with the glory that will be revealed in us." To grasp the meaning of this, imagine an old-fashioned scale—a fulcrum in the middle, a rod across the top, and a tray on either side hanging from chains. On one side of the scale is present suffering. On the other side is future pleasure. It's overwhelmingly lopsided. No matter how great today's suffering, it is outweighed more than a thousand to one by the glory, thrill, and excitement of future victory guaranteed by God.

Perhaps it is somewhat like the pain of childbirth, the strain of an athlete in competition, or the fear of the soldier in battle. The mother-to-be knows that after the pain comes the baby, and she's worth it. The athlete faces the strain with his eyes on the prize. The soldier endures the fear with the final victory in mind.

Today's suffering is never easy, but someday we'll look back from heaven's perspective and say, "It was all worth it."

Evidence of Christianity

In words a non-Christian can never understand, Peter wrote, "However, if you suffer as a Christian, do not be ashamed, but praise God that you bear that name" (1 Peter 4:16).

I think of American POWs and hostages who, in the midst of terrible abuse and torture and even death, never renounced their country. They suffered because they were Americans and were proud to do so.

Suffering because we bear the name of Jesus has far greater value, for such suffering proves we are Christians.

When the Romans tried to eliminate the early Christians from their empire, they did horrible things: they sent unarmed men and women into combat with armed gladiators, fed them to starving lions, drowned them, burned them alive at stakes, covered them with pitch and lighted them as lanterns to illumine their arenas. The testimony of history says that these believers sang hymns, prayed, and praised God as they died because suffering and dying for Christ was proof they were Christians.

It is hard to identify with either the Christians who went through such horrors or the suffering they endured. We doubt that we could be as heroic or faithful if confronted with similar torture, much less reason that martyrdom proved anything good. Personally, I believe that the grace from God for such situations comes only when we actually need it. We don't have what it takes to be courageously spiritual, but the Holy Spirit will give us the very help we need if that kind of suffering ever comes.

Claiming Comfort

God gives supernatural comfort to Christians because He is "the God of all comfort, who comforts us in all our troubles" (2 Corinthians 1:3–4). As Christians we can value suffering because of the supernatural comfort we would not receive if we didn't have troubles. Some may think this a masochistic approach, like the man who was asked why he hit himself on the head with a hammer. "Because it feels so good when I stop," he said.

The reality is that we live in a world riddled with suffering. No one is immune from illness, disappointment, hurt, or brokenness. The difference for the Christian is that such suffering is not the path to desperation. It is the channel of God's comfort.

I think of the comfort my wife, Charleen, has given to me. Her cool hand on my face has comforted me when I have been hot with fever. She has held me when I have cried with grief. It is not that I like the troubles, but I greatly value her comfort.

Even more, Christians value the comfort of God that suffering brings: the way He touches us with His hand or when He holds us close. His presence and power are wonderful. It is something that must be experienced to be understood because words are never good enough.

Glorifying God

Another value of Christian suffering that only a Christian can understand is the thrill of glorifying God.

Throughout history, efforts to kill off Christians have often won even more people to Jesus Christ because of the way Christians have suffered and died. When unbelievers see the power of Jesus Christ shining through those suffering, tortured, and martyred they conclude, "Those Christians die differently. They have something I don't have. I want what they've got."

The apostle Peter was a prime example. In John 21:18 Jesus predicted the way Peter would die: " 'I tell you the truth, when you were younger you dressed yourself and went where you wanted; but when you are old you will stretch out your hands, and someone else will dress you and lead you where you do not want to go.' " Realizing that these words might not make sense to readers, John added an explanation in the next verse: "Jesus said this to indicate the kind of death by which Peter would glorify God" (John 21:19).

Tradition says that Jesus' prediction was fulfilled when Peter was crucified in Rome, and that Peter asked to be crucified upside down because he was not worthy to die like Jesus.

Notice that the reason Jesus told Peter about his death was to show the opportunity Peter would have to "glorify God" in the way he died. Peter would suffer in a manner that would make God look good—that's what "glorify" means.

I've watched hundreds of people suffer through heartbreaks, shattered dreams, sickness, business failure, divorce, lost children, and more—suffering but demonstrating the power and presence of God in stunning ways. You could see, feel, and hear God in their lives. In their suffering, they glorified God.

Every Christian has the same opportunity when we suffer for any reason. We can make God look good by demonstrating Christian character, virtue, and grace that cannot be counterfeited. It really doesn't matter whether our suffering is the slight inconvenience in an otherwise wonderful life or the anguish of emotional and physical pain. In every suffering we can glorify God.

Does all this sound new, different, and strange to you? Read and study the Bible for yourself so that you understand the New Testament teaching on the value of suffering.

And then comes the great challenge: When suffering comes

to your life, don't run away. Don't curse the pain. Don't become bitter. In the reality of life's pains and problems, discover God himself. In the personal experience of suffering, experience the values of Jesus Christ.

Questions

For Thought:

1. If you are suffering right now, stop to consider whether it is because of sin, discipline, persecution, or some unknown source.
2. Have you ever been persecuted for your faith? How did you respond in that situation?
3. Would you be willing to suffer—or even die—to glorify God? Why or why not?

For Discussion:

1. Because God is our loving heavenly Father, He tells us in Hebrews that He will discipline us. Discuss some of the ways people are disciplined by God.
2. Sometimes we may never know the reason for our suffering. Job never did, but he steadfastly held to his integrity and trust in God. Are there ways we could encourage one another in times of suffering that utterly baffle us?
3. There is good in the pain of suffering that many passionately avoid. What are some of the benefits from suffering?

Chapter 14

In Touch With God

DO YOU THINK of America as a praying nation? If your answer is a strong "Yes!" you certainly agree with the pollsters' research! About 60% of Americans say they pray every day and 78% pray at least once a week. Only 1% of Americans say that they never pray.

Who do you think prays more, older adults or younger adults? If you answer "younger adults" you are right, according to the National Opinion Research Center based in Chicago. Adults born between 1939 and 1954 pray less on a daily basis than adults born between 1955 and 1970.

Prayer seems to increase in direct ratio to problems. Individuals and generations with greater problems tend to pray more.

Does prayer make a practical difference in life? In 1993, *Omni* magazine, citing research, stated that those who pray more have happier marriages.

Obviously prayer is considered valuable by a large segment of the population. But if prayer is so popular and powerful, why do so many people say they are not good at it, that they are weak and ignorant in prayer? Rarely, if ever, does anyone say, "I'm really good at praying!"

Prayer is like a lot of things that are both simple and complex, or at least start out to be simple and become more complex as you get further into them. One summer I worked as a camp counselor for junior boys in New York State. Every day the campers had archery lessons on the archery range. It was the one hour of the day when I had some peace and quiet, so I never went with them. They kept inviting and I kept declining. One day I said, "If you'll clean up everything in this cabin so it is perfect, I'll go with you to archery." To my amazement, they cleaned up, so I had to go. At the range they wanted me to shoot an arrow, which I refused to do because I didn't want to make a fool of myself. Again they insisted. I finally picked up a bow, chose and mounted the arrow, pulled back the string, carefully aimed, released the string, and hit the center of the bull's-eye. They were impressed! They asked me to do it again. I refused. I had used every bit of archery knowledge I had, which wasn't much, and lucked out. There are those who begin simply and buy more and more expensive and powerful bows, understand all about different types of arrows, practice for hours, test the wind, and consider a thousand other details I will never know or understand. It's the same way with hockey and baseball, with carpentry and chemistry, with writing and wrestling, and with prayer.

Prayer is very simple and easy when you start, but the further you get into it, the more there is to it. Just as runners start with a simple jog instead of a marathon, pray-ers begin with a simple prayer, not an all-night vigil.

Basics of Prayer

When Jesus taught His disciples how to pray, He said they should begin with "Our Father who art in heaven." These words indicate a relationship—a relationship between those who pray and God their father. Later Jesus told them that when they prayed they should be sure to mention His name. That's why we pray "In Jesus' name." So prayer is also based on a relationship with Jesus.

Everything about prayer is based on relationship. If there is no relationship, we're just talking to ourselves. The relationship may be good or bad, new or old, close or distant, warm or cold; but without that relationship there is no such thing as prayer.

"Caller ID" is a service that provides a read-out of the number and name of a caller before you answer your phone. If you have this service and the phone rings and the number and name of your very best friend appear, what are you most likely to do? Answer and talk, of course. What if the number and name are unfamiliar? You are less likely to answer, because communication is rooted in relationship.

Prayer is to relationship as swimming is to water. Without water you can't swim. You can pretend, but you can't swim. Without relationship there is no prayer. And since it is virtually impossible to have any kind of real relationship without communication, prayer is our communication link with God.

Prayer is not magic. It's not repeating memorized words. Prayer is multifaceted. Prayer is not just asking or just talking, nor is it limited to any mechanical formula or pattern. Like any other communication, prayer may be happy or sad, calm or emotional, reasonable or unreasonable, loud or silent.

Bible Prayers

The Bible's examples of prayer are many:

First Samuel 1:15 is the prayer of infertile Hannah who "was pouring out [her] soul to the LORD." She was so emotional that she was nearly kicked out of the temple because she appeared to be drunk.

In Psalm 88:1–2 the psalmist cries out for God to please listen: "O LORD, the God who saves me, day and night I cry out before you. May my prayer come before you; turn your ear to my cry."

Have you ever prayed and thought God was not listening? The Bible has many examples of pray-ers who thought God was ignoring them. "O LORD, hear my voice. Let your ears be attentive to my cry for mercy," prayed the psalmist on another occasion (Psalm 130:2).

What about complaining? It is, at times, a part of most relationships, including a relationship with God. Psalm 142:1–2 complains, "I cry aloud to the LORD; I lift up my voice to the LORD for mercy. I pour out my complaint before him; before him I tell my trouble." And Jeremiah 20:7 directly criticizes God: "O LORD, you deceived me, and I was deceived; you overpowered me and prevailed. I am ridiculed all day long; everyone mocks me."

Prayer, of course, includes asking: "Ask and it will be given to you; seek and you will find; knock and the door will be opened to you. For everyone who asks receives; he who seeks finds; and to him who knocks, the door will be opened" (Matthew 7:7–8). The apostle Paul assures us that this aspect of prayer is essential: "Do not be anxious about anything, but in everything, by prayer and petition, with thanksgiving, present your requests to God. And the peace of God, which transcends all understanding, will guard your hearts and your minds in Christ Jesus" (Philippians 4:6–7).

Sometimes praying is passionate, as described in Hebrews 5:7: "During the days of Jesus' life on earth, he offered up prayers and petitions with loud cries and tears to the one who could save him from death, and he was heard because of his reverent submission."

Sometimes praying is silent. Romans 8:26 describes those times when we just don't know what to pray and the Spirit does the praying for us. "In the same way, the Spirit helps us in our weakness. We do not know what we ought to pray, but the Spirit himself intercedes for us with groans that words cannot express."

Husbands and wives, parents and children, and best of friends have relationships that are multifaceted: sometimes passionate, sometimes silent; sometimes praising, sometimes pleading; sometimes comforting, sometimes complaining. In similar fashion, prayer communicates in many different ways, all within a relationship to God.

Belief in God

Of course all of this assumes a belief in God, for "without faith it is impossible to please God, because anyone who comes to him must believe that he exists and that he rewards those who earnestly seek him" (Hebrews 11:6).

It only makes sense that a prerequisite of prayer would be a belief in God. What would be the point in praying if we didn't believe God existed? Wouldn't that be like sending letters to Santa Claus when we know he is a myth? Yet researchers report that even atheists and agnostics pray! Sociologist Andrew Greeley suggests that their prayers are probably addressed "to whom it may concern."

We have all heard stories of non-Christians who prayed and received wonderful answers to their prayers. Many people have become Christians because they are convinced that God listened to their prayers.

This demonstrates the generosity of God! He will even hear the prayers of those who deny His existence. But there is a difference in the way God relates to the atheist, the agnostic, or the non-Christian. God hears and He may answer, but He has not obligated himself in advance. It is the difference between asking a stranger for a favor and asking a husband or wife. Marriage obligates us to another person in ways that we are not obligated to strangers. Thus, while God may graciously hear and even answer the prayers of those who are not believers, He has obligated himself to both hear *and* answer the prayers of those who believe in Him.

Beginning to Pray

The way to pray is to begin. Many people don't pray simply because they never get started. Some don't pray because they are afraid they won't do it right. But to think that prayer has to be done "right" is to misunderstand prayer.

Ask any parent about the "right way" for a child to call home and you will get a blank stare. Parents who love their children will tell you there is no "right way." They are glad to get the call day or night. They welcome calls that are long or short. Sons and daughters are welcome to call when they have nothing in particular to talk about and when they are facing the biggest crisis of life. It's okay to call Mom and Dad to tell a joke or just to cry, to dial direct or call collect. There just isn't a right way.

So when it comes to talking to God the Father, don't worry about getting it right. Just remember that He loves to hear from us—any time, any place, any topic. We can ask Him for money, plead for comfort, or just talk about what happened at the office during the day. Over the course of our life and our relationship with Him, our prayers will run the range of every emotion and touch on every issue. God has amazing tolerance. He understands. He welcomes our communication—He *wants* our communication. Just don't ignore Him. Don't miss out on Him. Don't treat Him as if He's not there or unimportant.

Sometimes we just go to God and let Him talk to us. We're upset and don't really know what to say.

In his book *Prayer*, Richard Foster tells the story of a man who took his two-year-old to the shopping mall. The child was irritated and irritating, fussing and fuming. Nothing worked to quiet him down.

The father picked up his son, held him close to his chest, and started to sing him an impromptu love song. There really was no tune, the father sang off-key, and nothing rhymed. But the child grew quiet and still, listening to his father's unusual song: "I love you. I'm so glad you're my boy. You make me happy. I like the way you laugh."

He sang to his son as he walked from one store to the next and all the way out to the car in the parking lot. When he finally stopped, as he was strapping the child into the seat, the little boy said, "Sing it to me again, Daddy! Sing it to me again!"[1]

Prayer is something like that. God scoops us up in His arms. He holds us and sings to us and tells us He loves us, and we may sing to Him and tell Him all about what is on our minds and in our hearts. And the more we experience this relationship with God through prayer, the more we keep saying, "Again, Father . . . let's do it again!"

Does Prayer Change Anything?

Millions of wall plaques have been hung on millions of walls proclaiming: "Prayer Changes Things." But is that true? Does it make any difference?

---

[1]Richard J. Foster, *Prayer* (New York: Harper Collins Publishers, 1992), 3–4.

Many would be quick to say, "If prayer doesn't change things, why bother praying? Isn't change the whole point of prayer?"

Before attempting to answer that basic question, let's think about it for a minute. Prayer is communion with God. Prayer is communication within relationship. Change is not primarily what prayer is all about. Prayer is about love and relationship with God.

Imagine a man and a woman who have just started dating. While at a party in his apartment, she sees a plaque on the wall that says "Marriage Changes Things." She laughs about it at first, but then discovers he is serious. She asks him what the plaque means.

"There are a lot of things in my life that I don't like and I want changed," he says. "I drink too much. I'm deeply in debt. I don't have a job. All of my former girlfriends are mad at me. I want to get married so all of those things can be changed, so that I can have what I want and be happy."

She is amazed at his ideas and asks, "What if marriage won't change the things you want changed?"

He replies, "Why would I bother to get married if marriage doesn't change the things I want changed?"

If she's smart she's out of there, no matter how attractive he may be. If or when she marries, she wants a husband who will marry her because he loves her, because he wants to be with her, because of their relationship—not because he wants changes (even though some or all of those changes might actually come with marriage).

God has feelings, too. He welcomes our prayers. But prayer is about love and relationship and communication—not making God into some kind of celestial genie in a bottle, there only to grant our wishes. Changes do result from a personal relationship with God, and prayer is an important means to those changes. But prayer would be a wonderful and glorious privilege even if nothing changed, because prayer is our means of connecting with God. Prayer is primarily about God, not primarily about change!

Understanding that change is secondary to what prayer is

about, let's tackle the question by breaking it down into four parts:

1. Does Prayer Change God?

In the fascinating story of King Hezekiah in 2 Kings 20:1–11, we learn that the prophet Isaiah had told Hezekiah he was going to die. When he heard the news, the king wept bitterly and prayed. Then Isaiah delivered this message to him from God: " 'I have heard your prayer and seen your tears; I will heal you. On the third day from now you will go up to the temple of the LORD. I will add fifteen years to your life' " (vv. 5–6).

This is no guarantee that God will grant an extra fifteen years to every terminal patient who prays. But in the case of Hezekiah that is exactly what God did. The same God who declared his impending death heard the king's prayer and added life. Prayer changed God.

But some theologians object, insisting that God never changes, using words like "immutable" and quoting Malachi 3:6, which says, "I the LORD do not change."

It is here that we cross over a line into the mysteries of God. Some assume that when prayer brings change it is because God had already chosen the change before we asked because He knew we would ask and He knew His answer would be yes. Others think that God leaves some options open, dependent on whether or not we ask. Still others believe that the person praying does the changing to fit what God has already decided.

The truth is, we don't know exactly *how* it works. But we do know that it works. People pray and God acts in ways that look a lot like change to us.

Hezekiah probably didn't get into such intricate arguments with the prophet Isaiah. As far as he was concerned, he prayed and God changed the prognosis—and that was good enough for him!

2. Does Prayer Change Circumstances?

Hezekiah would say, "Look no further! I prayed and God changed my circumstances!"

But we need not be limited to Hezekiah's experience, because God gives us this outright declaration in James 5:16–18:

> Therefore confess your sins to each other and pray for
> each other so that you may be healed. The prayer of a righ-
> teous man is powerful and effective.
> Elijah was a man just like us. He prayed earnestly that
> it would not rain, and it did not rain on the land for three
> and a half years. Again he prayed, and the heavens gave
> rain, and the earth produced its crops.

The clear teaching here is that the prayers of righteous persons are powerful and effective. A case in point is Elijah: when
he prayed, the weather changed.

I had a similar experience once. I stood with a farmer in a
muddy Colorado sugar beet field. It had rained for days. The
ground was soaked. More rain was forecast. The tractors
bogged down in the mud. Harvest was impossible. We prayed
for the rain to stop. That night the Denver TV weatherman said
that the system had unexpectedly changed and the forecast was
sunshine.

"Coincidence!" some would say. Perhaps. But, as an English
archbishop once said, "It's amazing how many coincidences occur when one begins to pray."[2]

3. Does Prayer Change Others?

Some of the most impassioned prayers are intercessory
prayers: prayers for change in someone else. Parents praying
for children. Wives praying for husbands. Husbands praying
for wives. Friends praying for friends. Prayers for churches and
companies and countries. Every day billions of prayers request
change in somebody else.

James 5:13–15 is very specific regarding this:

> Is any one of you in trouble? He should pray. Is anyone
> happy? Let him sing songs of praise. Is any one of you sick?
> He should call the elders of the church to pray over him
> and anoint him with oil in the name of the Lord. And the

---

[2]Bill Hybels, *Too Busy Not to Pray* (Downers Grove, Ill.: InterVarsity Press, 1988),
11.

prayer offered in faith will make the sick person well; the Lord will raise him up. If he has sinned, he will be forgiven.

Obviously the Bible answers yes to the question, "Does prayer change others?" In fact, the Bible commands us to pray for God to change others.

While I have witnessed and experienced both the prayers for and the changes in others, I also know that we must be careful to guard against any notion that our prayers can overrule either the will or sins of another person. Remember, in James 5:14 it is the person who is sick who requests the prayers of others.

God allows each person to make his or her own choices—even bad choices and sin. These choices may do terrible damage to others or enormous good. If people choose to murder, to live in immorality, to be abusive, or otherwise do what is wrong, we cannot force them to do right—even by prayer. They must choose to do right. However, we certainly can pray for God to put on the pressures that might lead them to choose what is best.

4. Does Prayer Change Me?

In practical terms, this may be the most important question of all: Does prayer change me? Jesus believed that the answer is another "yes!" On the night before He died, Jesus prayed a lot himself. When He took a break and talked to His three best friends, He said, "Pray so that you will not fall into temptation."

Jesus knew that life is a spiritual battlefield. Every Christian is threatened as if there were mines in the ground and bullets in the air. We are at risk to fall into temptation and be blown apart by sin. Praying for ourselves is the best protection. Not that the prayers themselves protect, but they are the means to deploy the greater forces of God himself.

I pray not to change God to do things my way but to change me to do things God's way. It is like taking a car in for wheel alignment. All the driving, turning, bumping, and hitting potholes throw the wheels out of alignment with the car's frame. But when I take it in to the garage, the technicians don't bend the frame to line up with the wheels; they adjust the wheels to line up with the frame. Every day I need to be realigned with

God: my thoughts with His thoughts, my will with His will, my life with His life. Yes . . . prayer changes me.

When We Pray

Change without Christ is worthless. Christ without change is impossible. So when we pray, we must center on Christ, not change. Seek Him more than the change in order to get the best of both.

Prayer is relational, not mechanical. Why is it that sometimes when the elders pray for the sick to be healed it works and sometimes it doesn't? Because all of prayer is woven into the complexities of relationship. It is not a mechanical transaction like pushing a button. When I push the elevator button once, I expect it to come. People are not like that. Saying "Come!" to a husband or wife is seldom a good approach. Relationships include time, intimacy, and reconciliation. Don't think of prayer as pushing God's button and demanding immediate results. Remember that prayer is connected to relationship with God.

And remember, answers come in "Yes," "No," and "Later." God is God, and He chooses who, how, and when to answer prayers for change.

God delights to do us good and give us good. When we pray, remember we are talking to our loving Father. He is always on our side.

Jesus strongly encouraged us to *ask* . . . and told us what to expect:

> "So I say to you: Ask and it will be given to you. . . .
> "Which of you fathers, if your son asks for a fish, will give him a snake instead? Or if he asks for an egg, will give him a scorpion? If you then, though you are evil, know how to give good gifts to your children, how much more will your Father in heaven." (Luke 11:9–13)

God the Father is better than the best of human fathers. He does not trick us. He will not harm us. He never seeks to give us evil. He is a wonderful father who delights to give us good.

The March 1994 *Life* magazine cover story on prayer mixed statistics ("Have your prayers ever been answered? Yes 95%")

with testimonials by a cross section of Americans, including United States Senator John McCain from Arizona, former Washington Redskins football coach Joe Gibbs, and twenty-four-year-old prostitute Geraldine Scott from Nevada. Perhaps the best statement on the value of prayer in everyday life came from ten-year-old Annah-Ruth Dominis of Sonoma, California:

> I pray in the morning; it's a family thing we do together. We sit around the table, close our eyes, and my mom and dad start off the prayer. We pray out loud for our day, that it will go well, and we pray for our President and people with troubles. At night I pray about my personal problems or I just talk to Him, telling Him about my day. I ask Him to help our vitamin business.
>
> My prayers are always answered with a yes, a no, a maybe or a wait. Nothing is really solved without God having something to do with it. My prayers about personal problems are answered with ideas that help to deal with them. I know God brought the ideas to me.
>
> Once, I just hadn't been really, totally nice to my sister. God told me to ask for her forgiveness. I was in bed. I wasn't even thinking about prayer or anything, but all of a sudden I heard this voice from heaven. God's voice is a voice that you really can't not obey. The Bible says God's voice is a still, small voice, but it's also stern and loud and commanding. When He told me to apologize to my sister, I said, "O.K., God, I'll do it in the morning." And He goes, "No. Now." So I got out of bed and went and did it.[3]

---

[3]*Life* (March 1994), 62.

Questions

For Thought:

1. Jesus taught that the basis of prayer is relationship with God. How is your prayer life affected by your relationship with God?
2. Why should prayer make a practical difference in your life?
3. Do you find it hard to pray? Why?

For Discussion:

1. Prayer is primarily about love and relationship with God, not about change. Why do most of us pray to get God to change our circumstances instead of availing ourselves of the privilege of a relationship with Him?
2. Romans 8:26 teaches us that at times "the Spirit himself intercedes for us with groans that words cannot express." What do you believe this means? Tell about a time you experienced this kind of prayer.
3. Talk about some ways to simply begin a prayer life: following a thirty-day devotional, finding a prayer partner, joining a church prayer group?
4. Since God has feelings and welcomes our prayers, how do you think our prayers affect Him?

Chapter 15

Putting Values Together

THE MOVIE *Indecent Proposal,* starring Robert Redford and Demi Moore, was more than a top box-office attraction in 1993. It was *the* topic of talk shows and coffee breaks across North America. The film raises a provocative moral dilemma when a very wealthy man offers one million dollars to spend the night with another man's wife.

It was not the movie as much as the moral questions at the heart of it that fascinated so many people. How much is a marriage worth? Are women to be bought and sold by rich men and husbands? But the real question everyone debated was, "Would you do it if you had the opportunity?" If you were rich enough, would you pay a million dollars to bed another man's wife? If you weren't rich, would you prostitute your wife for a million dollars? If you were a woman at the center of such an indecent proposal, would you agree if the price were high enough? The fantasies of millions of Americans played the game.

What is really at issue here is *integrity.* For great financial gain would we go against what we believe to be right?

When researchers James Patterson and Peter Kim wrote *The*

Day America Told the Truth, they asked people a similar question: "What are you honestly willing to do for $10 million?"

- 25% said they would abandon their entire family.
- 25% would abandon their church.
- 23% would become prostitutes for a week or more.
- 7% would kill a stranger.[1]

The next time you're in a crowd of 100 people, try to figure out which 7 of them would kill you for the right price. Out of every 1,000 there are 70, and in a metropolitan area or state with a population of 4 million there could be about 280,000 murderers for hire if the price is right.

Patterson and Kim did a follow-up survey, asking the same people if they would do the same things for less money. At $5 million, $4 million, and $3 million the answers were pretty much the same. Below $2 million there was a falloff in what people would agree to do, leading the authors to conclude that "our price in America seems to be $2 million or thereabouts."[2]

What wrong do you think a Christian would do for enough money? Or do you think Christians value integrity more than anything the world can offer?

What Is Integrity?

The old *Candid Camera* TV show had an episode where an apartment was advertised for a very affordable rent. Prospective renters were shown around the luxury unit by rental agents until they would ask, "Where is the bathroom?" The agent then answered, "This apartment doesn't have a bathroom, which really saves a lot of space." The reactions of the prospective renters were classic as they expressed their disbelief that there could be a luxury apartment without a bathroom. One lady, after host Allan Funt said, "You're on *Candid Camera,*" asked, "Yeah, I understand that, but where *is* the bathroom?"

That apartment wasn't consistent. It wasn't complete.

[1]James Patterson and Peter Kim, *The Day America Told the Truth* (New York: NAL-Dutton, 1992).
[2]Ibid., 65–66.

Something that should obviously be there wasn't. It lacked integrity.

Integrity has played a significant role in the business concepts of Total Quality Management and Zero Defect Manufacturing. Who wants a heart pacemaker that works most of the time? Who values an airplane with 90% of the systems operating? Who hires a surgeon who sutures so well that the scar is nearly invisible but who tends to leave scissors inside the patient?

Integrity brings all of life together into a consistent whole. When each part of a person's life agrees with every other part, when everything is there that is supposed to be there, that person has integrity.

For the Christian, integrity is more than God, truth, salvation, godliness, faith, fellowship, love, prayer, evangelism, suffering, and good works. Integrity is none of these. Integrity is all of these.

Christian integrity isn't faith without good works. It isn't loyalty to God when life is easy but disloyalty when life includes suffering. It is not telling the truth at home but lying at work. It can never be saying that we believe the Bible and then disobeying what the Bible says.

Christian integrity is total Christianity. It is Zero Defect Living.

Immediately some say, "That's impossible! We're still sinners. We can't live with total consistency and zero defects." You're right! Just as there is no such thing as Zero Defect pacemakers or airplanes. But no one would dare to seek anything less, nor tolerate defects once they have been discovered.

Christians are not perfect because human beings cannot be perfect, but we can still value integrity—because God values integrity. We can still do our best to see that all the values of Christianity come together with consistency in every area of our lives.

If we need an example, Psalm 15 describes the person of integrity:

> He whose walk is blameless
>   and who does what is righteous,

who speaks the truth from his heart
   and has no slander on his tongue,
who does his neighbor no wrong
   and casts no slur on his fellow man,
who despises a vile man
   but honors those who fear the LORD,
who keeps his oath
   even when it hurts,
who lends his money without usury
   and does not accept a bribe against the innocent.
He who does these things
   will never be shaken.

Integrity is much more than a definition or a description. It is a call for self-evaluation: "Is my life integrated or segregated?"

Self-Evaluation

The segregated life is divided into separate and disconnected departments. This is the person who has a home life, a church life, a business life, a private life, a public life—and who believes and behaves differently in each.

When life is segregated, different parts operate by different values. It is heard in the voices of those who say, "You should never operate the church like a business," and "There's no place for religion in the workplace." It is the philosophy of those who would never have pornography around their homes but regularly indulge in it on business trips. It is the man who is proud of keeping his word in business deals but does not keep his marriage vows. It is the woman who condemns sexual harassment and racial discrimination at her company but fights to keep minorities out of her neighborhood. It is the couple who are generous in their giving to the church but underpay their employees in the family business.

You get the picture: Segregation is the opposite of integration and integration is central to integrity. Historically many Christians have viewed Christianity as a "seamless garment" where every part is connected to every other part without divisions. Thus, the Christian's life is to be a smooth and uninterrupted continuity between all beliefs and practices and relationships.

An interesting line in Proverbs 10:9 says, "The man of integrity walks securely." I think we could add that the person without integrity walks stressfully. It is very stressful to live life compartmentally and inconsistently, operating with different values for different segments of life.

When I think of integrity, I always think of Job. Actually, Job is most famous for his suffering, when he should be most famous for his integrity. That was God's observation in that rare conversation He had with Satan. Job 2:3 reports that "the LORD said to Satan, 'Have you considered my servant Job? There is no one on earth like him; he is blameless and upright, a man who fears God and shuns evil. And he still maintains his integrity.' " God was proud of Job because he didn't change his values when he lost his family and his fortune. He was a man of integrity.

Satan then zapped Job with a terrible, painful illness that racked his body. Job's wife told him to change his values when life became so hard. She asked him, "Are you still holding on to your integrity? Curse God and die!" (Job 2:9).

Mrs. Job had plenty of company. Most of Job's friends told him he was wrong to stay consistent to his values when everything was turning bad. He had a right to change when life dumped on him. After long dialogue, however, he made his position clear: "Till I die, I will not deny my integrity" (Job 27:5).

Job valued integrity. He was a whole man, consistent, every value connected to every other value, undaunted by the changing circumstances in his life.

Job made a choice that every Christian needs to make, regardless of whether we evaluate our present lives to be integrated or segregated.

Which Life Operating System?

Those who work with computers know the importance of "operating systems." It is the operating system that makes a computer work. No matter how powerful the chip or how sophisticated the hardware, it can't do anything without an operating system.

The system one chooses determines all else that follows. Those strange combinations of initials are very important—like MS DOS for "Microsoft Disc Operating System" and AMOS for "Alpha Micro Disc Operating System."

As I understand it, a choice must be made. A computer can't operate on all operating systems nor repeatedly switch around or run software incompatible with the operating system chosen.

This suggests many parallels in life. We must all choose a "Life Operating System." Those who become Christians switch from a "Sin Operating System" or "Self Operating System" to what might be called JC LOS or a "Jesus Christ Life Operating System."

With our operating system comes a whole set of values, and if we are going to function well, we cannot choose some of these values and not others. It doesn't work well to try to mix the JC LOS system with any other system—they are mutually exclusive. When Jesus Christ operates our lives, we become incompatible with a lot of programs. And when we are Christians, we can run whole new programs never before dreamed possible. The truth of it is that the hardware of our lives and bodies were designed to be run by Jesus. And when we are fully up and running, we value and have integrity—all of life and all of Christ's values consistently running together.

Another way of saying this—a way very familiar to older generations—is to say that we live under "the Lordship of Jesus Christ." He runs our lives.

Matthew 6:24 says it even better, comparing a Christ operating system to a money operating system: "No one can serve two masters. Either he will hate the one and love the other, or he will be devoted to the one and despise the other. You cannot serve both God and Money." (Any other operating system could be substituted for money. We cannot serve God and Sex, God and Power, God and Self, God and Business, God and Anything.)

As Christians, we choose Jesus Christ to operate our lives. As Christians we value Jesus Christ running all of our lives; we value integrity.

Living by Choices More Than Circumstances

Everyone's life is impacted by circumstances we don't control. We cannot choose our parents, control the behavior of other people, or exempt ourselves from the unexpected. Unfortunately, too many people assume that circumstances control life and we are either good-luck winners or bad-luck losers. This defective, fatalistic philosophy has contributed to the victim mentality of an entire generation.

Fatalism is not a doctrine of Christianity. We accept the certainty of circumstances but also exercise the responsibility of human choice. The percentages vary from person to person, but the norm is probably 10% of life controlled by circumstances and the remaining 90% determined by our response. This is obvious when we compare persons with similar circumstances who handle them in opposite ways—one for defeat and the other for victory.

Integrity is living Christianly because it is the right and best thing to do no matter what our circumstances. The choices of the Christian life are determined by the values we have learned from God, not the circumstances that happen to us. Wouldn't it be great if we moved the emphasis from "What happened to you?" to "How did you respond?"

A fascinating example of this kind of integrity appeared in a paid advertisement in a Nairobi, Kenya, newspaper, *The East African Standard:*

> ALL DEBTS TO BE PAID
> I ALLAN HARANGUI ALIAS WANIEK HARANGUI, of P.O. Box 40380, Nairobi, have dedicated services to the Lord Jesus Christ. I must put right all my wrongs. If I owe any debt or damage personally or any of the companies I have been director or partner i.e.
> GUARANTEED SERVICES LTD.
> WATERPUMPS ELECTRICAL AND GENERAL CO. SALES AND SERVICES
> Please contact me or my advocates J.K. Kibicho and Company, Advocates, P.O. Box 73137, Nairobi for a settlement. No amount will be disputed.

GOD AND HIS SON JESUS CHRIST BE GLORI-
FIED.[3]

Now there is a man who values integrity. Like Job, no matter
what the cost, he wants all of life to hang together, consistently,
operated by and for Jesus Christ.

Questions

For Thought:

1. How deep is your commitment to maintaining integrity?
2. Do you believe your life is integrated, or does it feel frag-
   mented?
3. Do you find life stressful? How might you be causing some
   of that stress by compartmentalizing your life and living inconsistently?
4. Ask God to show you how to truly "be yourself" in every
   situation.

For Discussion:

1. Imagine a situation in which a Christian might—for a high
   enough price—choose to violate his or her own conscience
   in order to alleviate some stressful situation. How would
   such a choice cause even *more* stress in the long run than the
   person was trying to alleviate in the first place?
2. All of us know people who have responded to difficult life
   circumstances in victorious ways rather than focusing on
   their misfortunes. Share together some testimonies of people
   you have met who have overcome great obstacles. What part
   does faith play in their choices?
3. How can we encourage one another to live with integrity?

---

[3]R. Kent Hughes, *Disciplines of a Godly Man* (Wheaton, Ill.: Crossway Books,
1991), 126–127.

Chapter 16

Does Jesus Trust You?

IT WAS A dark day for Christians in Smyrna. The year was A.D. 155 and the persecutions were increasing across the Roman Empire. The proconsul had even issued an arrest order for Polycarp, the nearly one-hundred-year-old bishop of the ancient Asian city.

When the soldiers brought the bishop into the city arena, he stood before a wild and hostile crowd. Thirsty for his blood, they shouted for his death. But the proconsul wanted to give the old man a last chance to recant. Hushing the crowd, he called on Polycarp to curse the Christ and live.

Polycarp answered: "Eighty and six years I have served Him and He has done me no wrong. How then dare I blaspheme my King who has saved me?"

At that, the proconsul gave the signal to execute, and the bishop died a martyr.

Polycarp lived at a time when the culture around him was as heathen and hostile to Christians as any in history. Yet he was not controlled from the outside by his culture but from the inside by his values. He lived Christianly. He died Christianly.

What enabled that old man to remain faithful to Jesus Christ even in the face of the executioner's sword? Where did he learn the values that enabled him to both trust Christ *and* to be trustworthy?

Surely Polycarp's secret was learned from his spiritual mentor, the apostle John. John had a unique relationship with Jesus Christ. Thousands thronged Jesus and hundreds followed Him, but only a dozen were called disciples. And of that dozen, three formed an inner circle. Only one, however, was "the disciple whom Jesus loved": Jesus' best friend, John.

Understanding this special relationship between Jesus and John helps us understand how Polycarp lived and died Christianly in the middle of the second century, and how we can live and die Christianly at the turn of a millennium into the twenty-first century.

John Trusted Jesus

From beginning to end, the relationship of John to Jesus was full of trust.

Enough to Forsake Prosperity

The biblical data clearly indicates that John was a man of means. Mark 1:20 speaks of the "hired men" who worked in the family fishing business owned by John's father, Zebedee. While the fishing business was up north in Galilee, John 19:27 indicates that John had a house down south in Jerusalem. According to John 18:15, he knew the high priest well enough to have free access to his courtyard and home.

When these pieces are put together, it becomes apparent that John had servants in an era of poverty, a family-owned business when there wasn't much of a middle class, a second home in the city, and a personal acquaintance with one of the most famous and powerful men in the nation. But John gave it all up for Jesus.

One day Jesus invited John to join His little band. John quickly sensed that this man was worth following: He was different; He spoke like no other man John had ever heard; the power of God was in Him in a way that not even John the Baptist could claim. I doubt that on that first day John fully understood all that trusting Jesus would mean. He had not yet heard the Master's call to radical discipleship, nor could he possibly anticipate the fear that would grip him in the Garden of Gethsemane on the eve of Jesus' death. John probably couldn't have explained why, but he just trusted Jesus. It was a simple trust, yet strong enough to cause him to walk away from servants and a fishing business and a second home and highly placed friends.

John reminds me of William Borden, the young Yale graduate who left behind the extraordinary wealth of the Borden Milk Company in order to become a missionary to the all-but-unknown Hindus of Egypt. He reminds me of others I've known who have been willing to leave family businesses, lucrative professions, and great power in order to follow Jesus Christ.

To those who trust Jesus, none of this seems like much of a sacrifice. John, like Polycarp, knew that Jesus would do him "no wrong," that Jesus was absolutely trustworthy.

Enough to Risk His Life

John was the only male disciple who showed up at the crucifixion. The women were there, perhaps because their courage was greater or their risk was less. No doubt the risk was high for John. All of his colleagues were holed up in a secret place with the door locked, hoping to escape association with the Messiah whom they had followed for three years. They thought that the animosity toward Jesus could quickly spill over to them and that they would be crucified as well.

I cannot believe that John understood so much better than the others. His theology was as embryonic and his emotions as confused as theirs. It's just that he loved and trusted Jesus enough to risk his life, even when Jesus wasn't very lovely and when all the external causes for trust had been stripped away.

It is easy to trust a leader who is walking on water or preaching scintillating sermons to crowds of thousands. It is quite another matter to love and trust a leader who is naked, bleeding, and being mocked by important people. John trusted Jesus even when He didn't look like He was worth trusting—and even when John's own life was at risk.

At the one hundredth anniversary of the arrival of missionaries in Zaire, Christians gathered to celebrate from that part of Zaire once called the Belgian Congo. The festivities lasted all day with music, preaching, food, and conversations. Many reminisced about the early days and praised God for the progress of the Gospel and the church.

Near the end of the long program, a very old man stood to give a speech. He said that he soon would die and that he needed to tell something that no one else knew. If he didn't tell, his secret would go with him to his grave. He explained that when the first white missionaries came, his people didn't know whether to believe their message or not. So they devised a plan to slowly and secretly poison the missionaries and watch them die. One by one children and adults became ill, died, and were buried. It was when his people saw how these missionaries died that they decided to believe their message.

Think of it—those missionaries never knew what was happening. They didn't know they were being poisoned and they didn't know why they were dying. They didn't know they were martyrs. They stayed and died because they trusted Jesus. And it was the way they died that taught others how to live.

Just like John. He trusted Jesus enough to risk his life on crucifixion day.

Enough to Stay Anonymous

Maybe you have never thought of John's anonymity as an expression of trust. Never once throughout the twenty-one chapters of his famous gospel does he call himself by name. He always refers to "the other disciple" or "the disciple Jesus loved" but never "John." Even though we refer to the fourth book of the New Testament as "The Gospel According to St. John," he never called it that. Originally the book had no name, and the title was later added by editors.

John trusted Jesus to make him famous or to keep him obscure, but he never thought of that as his choice to make. He trusted Jesus to fulfill his dreams and to give him self-esteem.

He chose not to promote himself but chose instead to promote the Lord whom he loved, followed, served, and trusted.

That is an example worth following today when we are so tempted to self-promotion and to seek fame. John wanted to just live Christianly, trusting Jesus to decide the rest.

Jesus Trusted John

It is wonderful the way John trusted Jesus enough to forsake prosperity, risk his life, and stay anonymous, but that is not what is most amazing about their relationship. The front-page news is not that John trusted Jesus but that Jesus trusted John.

With His Gospel

The last two verses of John's gospel say,

> This is the disciple who testifies to these things and who wrote them down. We know that his testimony is true.
> Jesus did many other things as well. If every one of them were written down, I suppose that even the whole world would not have room for the books that would be written. (John 21:24–25)

Most of the disciples did not write gospels. And most of the gospels that were written did not make it into the New Testament. John's is the fourth and final gospel to be written and incorporated into the Bible. It is very different from Matthew, Mark, and Luke, purposely adding to Jesus' biography that which the others did not include.

Why John? Because Jesus trusted John to get the story straight. Jesus trusted John to include what was essential and to exclude what was unnecessary. It was no small task since there was enough material to fill the whole world with books.

Because Jesus trusted John, He included him in the inner circle of three disciples, brought him along to the top of the Mount of Transfiguration while most of the rest waited at the bottom, and had John sit close enough to hear the whispers of Judas' betrayal at the Last Supper (John 13:23–26). It's all in the gospel John wrote.

What an overwhelming trust. Jesus knew John could be counted on, that John would represent Jesus well, and that John would pen the gospel as the gospel needed to be written. Today, we can quote "For God so loved the world that he gave his one and only Son, that whoever believes in him shall not perish but have eternal life" (John 3:16) because John was worthy of Jesus' trust.

With His Love

John is called the disciple whom Jesus loved (John 19:26). How could any one person be described that way? It implies that Jesus loved John more than the others—that John was Jesus' best friend. A best friend is someone with whom we share laughter and pain and secrets. Most of all, a best friend is someone we trust more than any other person in the world.

There was a danger, however, in being chosen to be Jesus' best friend. Imagine what such a relationship could do to a person's life. Imagine the enormous pressure to take pride in that relationship. If Jesus identified someone as His best friend today, we would probably expect that person to travel around the world, give speeches, write books, make a movie, and hold seminars. It could be a very profitable enterprise.

There would also be a temptation to abuse the relationship, asking Jesus for special favors or access to His knowledge and power. There would be the temptation to look down on other Christians as less loved.

But Jesus knew that John could be trusted with His special friendship and that he would neither abuse it nor be destroyed by it.

With His Mother

Protestants don't often make much of Mary the mother of Jesus. Yet she was obviously a great concern to the Savior in the final moments of His crucifixion:

> Near the cross of Jesus stood his mother, his mother's sister, Mary the wife of Clopas, and Mary Magdala. When Jesus saw his mother there, and the disciple whom he loved

standing nearby, he said to his mother, "Dear woman, here
is your son," and to the disciple, "Here is your mother."
From that time on, this disciple took her into his home.
(John 19:25–27)

Jesus needed help. His hands and feet were nailed and His
life was soon to end. Crucifixion usually brings death by as-
phyxiation—the chest muscles become paralyzed, making it extremely difficult to exhale. Victims on crosses don't talk much
because they don't have the breath. That's one of the reasons
Jesus spoke only seven times during the whole crucifixion or-
deal. When He did speak, His words were few and what He said
was very important.

According to Jewish custom of that day, as the oldest son of
a widow Jesus was responsible for His mother's care until she
died. But He couldn't take care of her when He was nailed to
the cross, nor would He be around for her after His death. He
needed someone He could trust to take care of His mother. He
chose John.

When Peter and the other apostles fled Jerusalem under persecution, John stayed behind—to take care of Mary. When the
others were spreading the Good News to distant lands, John
was still back in Jerusalem. Tradition says he stayed there until
Mary died and he had fulfilled his trust.

Does Jesus Trust You?

As a Christian you've probably been asked ten thousand
times if you trust Jesus. I hope that your answer is a resounding
"Yes!" We talk a great deal about trusting Jesus for problems,
opportunities, health, marriage, family, job, church, and everything else. That's the way it should be because Jesus is trustworthy and He wants us to trust Him. We should trust Him
enough to forsake prosperity, risk life, stay anonymous, and
give Him the fame. He is trustworthy! But are we?

Who can Jesus trust? He needs disciples to take on a broad
range of modern assignments. He needs those who will demonstrate His presence and power in a myriad of situations and
circumstances. He needs followers who will live Christianly—
not just in the easy circumstances, but in all circumstances.

Who can Jesus trust with difficult employment? He has lots of volunteers for easy assignments with good salary and generous benefits. But who will serve Him in the hard places?

Who can Jesus trust with a rebellious son or daughter? Jesus has a long list of volunteers willing to parent perfect children with straight teeth, straight *A*'s, and straight sexual orientation. Who can He trust to live Christianly with children who aren't so perfect?

Who can Jesus trust with recurring cancer? Who will be His disciple to live a painful life and show the world how to be faithful to Jesus even in suffering and death?

The list goes on and on. Jesus needs disciples He can trust to live Christianly in small homes and large mansions, with high-paying jobs and with unemployment, with prominent political office and obscure anonymity, with singleness and marriage, with parenthood and infertility, with spectacular answers to prayer and with no answer to prayer.

The values war will not be won on the picket lines or in the halls of Congress. The values war can only be won as Christians live out all the Christian values in all the circumstances of life.

Who can Jesus trust to live out Christian values in a changing culture? Can He trust you?

Questions

For Thought:

1. Ask yourself if you trust Jesus enough to believe that whatever your life circumstances, He has chosen this place for you to be His disciple.
2. After studying this book, have you changed your answer to the question asked earlier: How can I live Christianly in my present circumstances?
3. What makes you believe Jesus can trust you enough to for-

sake prosperity for yourself, to stay anonymous and not seek your own honor, or to risk your life for His sake?

For Discussion:

1. How have any of your attitudes about values changed as a result of reading this book and talking together? Share some examples.
2. How have you been challenged to live more Christianly?
3. What experiences have you had in these last few weeks that illustrate or emphasize some of the lessons on values that we have been discussing?
4. Pray for one another for God's grace to live according to His values and to resist the values that the world offers.